THE WAY HOME
A Wilderness Odyssey

THE WAY HOME

A Wilderness Odyssey

BIBI WEIN

TUPELO PRESS

The Way Home: A Wilderness Odyssey
Copyright © 2004 Bibi Wein
ISBN 1-932195-13-0
Printed in Canada

First paperback edition October 2004
Library of Congress Control Number: 2004104641

Tupelo Press PO Box 539, Dorset, Vermont 05251
802.366.8185 • web www.tupelopress.org

Grateful acknowledgment is made to the following for permission to reprint
excerpts from previously published material:

Excerpt from "East Coker" in *Four Quartets,* ©1940 by T.S. Eliot and renewed
1968 by Esme Valerie Eliot, reprinted by permission of Harcourt, Inc. and Faber
and Faber Ltd., London.

Possession, ©1990, A.S. Byatt, reprinted by permission of Random House, Inc.

"Lost" by David Wagoner, ©1972, reprinted by permission of the author.

Tracks in the Wilderness of Dreaming, Robert Bosnak, ©1996, Delacorte Press,
reprinted by permission of the author

"The Old Pine Tree," by Jeanne Robert Foster, from *Adirondack Portraits: A Piece
of Time,* edited by Noel Riedinger-Johnson, Syracuse University Press, 1986.

Contested Terrain: A New History of Nature and People in the Adirondacks, Philip
G. Terrie, ©1997, reprinted by permission of The Adirondack Museum.

From Where We Stand: Recovering a Sense of Place, ©1993, Deborah Tall, Johns
Hopkins University Press, reprinted by permission of the author.

Cover and text designed by William Kuch, WK Graphic Design
Cover Art: Laura Von Rosk, *Hidden Road,* oil on wood, 2003

*Tupelo Press is an award-winning independent literary press that publishes
fine fiction, non-fiction and poetry books. It is a registered 501(c)3 non-profit
organization and relies on the support of literature lovers to carry out its
mission of publishing extraordinary writing.*

for Bob
with love and gratitude for all the
years on the trail

and for my father
whose love of literature was my
earliest inspiration

In the middle, not only in the middle of the way
But all the way, in a dark wood, in a bramble,
On the edge of a grimpen where is no secure foothold,
And menaced by monsters, fancy lights
Risking enchantment.

East Coker, T. S. Eliot

PART I

Into the Wild Wood

*There once was a poor shoemaker
who had...a useless, hopeless,
dreaming daughter, to whom her
mother would often say that she
should try to fend for herself in the
wild wood, and then she would know
the value of listening to advice, and of
doing things properly. And this filled
the perverse daughter with a great
desire to go even a little way into the
wild wood, where there were no plates
and no stitching, but might well be a
need of such things as she knew she
had it in herself to perform...*

Possession, A.S. Byatt

1

Somewhere around the age of forty, when I should have been deciding if I wanted to take my last chance at having a second child, should have been looking for a good job to replace the one that had recently ended (and later to replace the terrible one I wandered into), I began instead to learn everything I could about staying out all night in the woods.

Since I lived in Manhattan, this pursuit could hardly be construed as even marginally relevant to my real life. But I'd recently acquired a life apart from my "real" one—a life lived outdoors, if mostly in my mind. It was a little like being in love with someone unavailable and possibly dangerous, with whom one can never spend enough time. Though one may crave the dailiness of a life with such a lover and believe oneself devoted to discerning his elusive truths, what's essential to the obsession is that his naked face remains unseen.

Such was my romance with the forest: neither concrete nor entirely abstract, but an amalgam of sensual experience and blind desire, driven by myth, emotion and imagination.

When I caught myself striding through the noonday crowds near Rockefeller Center wondering whether the perfume I'd dabbed at my neck this morning would attract bears, I realized I was, as much as any bigamist, straddling two worlds.

Yet, in both my indoor life and my mostly imagined outdoor one, I had one partner. Timid in our early emotional explorations as we nursed recent wounds, we devoted much of our first year together to wandering on foot in unfamiliar terrain. After a few dinner-and-movie dates, I'd suggested to Bob that we take a walk in a state park one Sunday—and it was as if I'd tripped a latch and released him from a cage.

We went wandering only once or twice a month at first. Bob was a classical clarinetist with a day job in a music store; I was juggling free-lance writing assignments with a full-time job in the video industry. We both frequently worked weekends. But the urge to rush out, rain or shine, to the wildest places we could reach within a day's round-trip of Manhattan was a passion, mutual and unexpected. Neither of us had done anything like this before, and it seemed pretty peculiar to our respective friends. Until now, smoky jazz clubs had been our natural habitat.

It was in a bar, in fact, that we met. But it was nature that brought us together.

It was a rainy Sunday night in May, a shaky six months after I'd left my long marriage. I'd been visiting a writer friend in Soho and, after a rather tense discussion of our respective works in progress, we decided to go out for a drink—at the nearest possible place, because it was raining so hard. My friend suggested the small bar of a trendy restaurant across the street from her apartment. The place was empty except for two bearded men seated at the bar. They eagerly turned our way, but we wrote them off at once. One was not tall enough—I was still looking for some replica of my 6'2" ex, and my friend was nearly a six-footer herself—and the other was too old. Choosing seats as far from the men as we could get in this tiny place, we rebuffed their attempts to strike up conversation, and ignored them when they moved closer. After about an hour, though, I heard the younger, shorter man—who was now seated right next to me—telling his companion about watching cardinals carrying food to each other in his parents' backyard. Intrigued to hear a man in New York City talking about birds, I turned, finally, to look at him. I saw that he had with him a music stand, and a copy of *The Golden Bough*. He also had blue eyes steady and clear as morning, even though he'd had a bit to drink, and a face I'd be happy to look at for the rest of my life. *Tall enough,* I decided, watching his slender form disappear into the darkness as he headed for the rest room. When he returned, we went off to a jazz club called Bradley's to get better acquainted. His kiss as we said good night in the back of a cab was long and complicated, and full of all kinds of possibilities, including tenderness.

"I'll cook you a chicken," he said, the first time he invited me to his apartment. The windows of his tiny top floor walkup at a ragged edge of Greenwich Village were filled with lush hanging plants, the exposed brick walls lined with books and record albums and music scores. It looked like home.

Before long we were exploring the Kittatiny Mountains and New Jersey's Highlands, the Pine Barrens, the Catskills, the Appalachian Trail. The more formidable the hike, the better Bob liked it. I was less ambitious and soon persuaded him to slow down and look around. Still, if we got down from whatever mountain we were climbing with an hour of daylight to spare, he'd get cranky if we couldn't climb another. The late glow of afternoon often found us arguing about where we had to turn back in order to be out of the forest before dark. Bob always wanted to push further. I, playing the realist, usually prevailed, and as the light grew dimmer he'd reluctantly admit that we couldn't have covered all the ground he'd proposed before night set in.

Together, we learned to read the land. As children, we'd both lived urban lives that had included neither summer camp nor much in the way of family vacations. But we each brought to our adventures a few bits of knowledge. I'd spent the last decade of my newly defunct marriage on eastern Long Island, in a house that backed onto a scrubby wood. These woods had become my place of solitary wandering and solace in difficult times. I'd done enough rambling to learn the names of a few plants and birds; but little remained truly wild in the area apart from water: the ocean, which terrified me, and the placid bays where, repeatedly, I'd failed to learn to swim. It was the few hikes I'd taken with friends after returning to Manhattan that had taught me the most rudimentary facts about trails and blazes, and given me my first tantalizing taste of deep forests into which, I imagined, one might climb forever.

Bob had grown up in a cold water flat in Paterson, New Jersey, that happened to be directly across the street from a spectacular and famous waterfall, where he'd done some daredevil explorations among the rocks. He'd seen some formidable wilderness during his military time as a bandsman in Alaska, and knew a bit of geology and a lot about the sky. So between us we had a rudimentary cosmology—Bob conversant with what was above and below, and me with some idea of what was in between. But this was not enough to keep us out of trouble. We got lost a lot and had some close calls.

The first time we got lost might have terminally soured our relationship, had we not found our way back on track in a few minutes. Sunday outings were timed to get me back in Manhattan to meet the Hampton Jitney, on which my 12-year-old daughter Elizabeth returned from weekends with her father. On this day, Bob and I were negotiating a confusing network of trails in a park quite close to the city. I thought we were on our way out when we realized we'd wasted half an hour on the wrong trail and had been walking in circles. Bob insisted, however, that he knew the correct way now—and indeed, he did. The bus was late and we were early and all was well.

Much more serious, however, was a bright Saturday in early December when we carelessly wandered from a popular hiking route in search of a lake. Surprise Lake. On the map, a trail went right to it. Out in the woods, the path, marked sporadically by a splotch of faded orange paint on a tree, was all but obliterated by blueberry and bramble. We didn't find the lake, and by nightfall, we were lost on a ridgetop in an ice storm. Having no flashlight or matches, we were extremely lucky to make our way back to the car in a couple of hours. After that, we always carried emergency supplies, including flashlights, waterproof matches and a pair of "space blankets"—each a large, virtually weightless sheet of mylar folded into a cellophane package about the size of a dinner roll. Thus prepared to spend an impromptu night in the woods, we'd never had to.

A decade later, we were very much at home in the forests of the northeast, and had much more time to spend in them. When my daughter made a smooth transition from college to graduate school with a full fellowship, I'd felt free to take the financial risks of full-time freelancing so that I'd have more time for my own writing. Bob's early love of science had been reawakened in our wanderings and, frustrated with both his dead-end job and the financial insecurity of the music world, he'd begun a second master's degree and a new career as a high school science teacher. And we'd purchased a tiny cabin near the heart of the Adirondack Mountains in upstate New York, a region so rugged and remote even native Americans never settled there, and New Englanders referred to it as "the bush" until well into the nineteenth century.

Long before we became second-home-owners, the Adirondacks had become our second home. We'd spent nearly every vacation and holiday and long weekend in some part of the six-million-acre state park for years. Still, one midsummer evening about a year after we'd bought the cabin, we went for a short walk before dinner and didn't come back for a very long time.

"Take the compass," I called to Bob, as he slung his camera over his shoulder. I was darting from room to room hunting for my ever-missing glasses. Having wasted ten minutes before I found them, I snatched my pack from a hook and hastily checked to see what was inside. At the bottom, a thin nylon windbreaker lay matted in a sticky ball. I left it (rain was forecast), considered tossing in a sweater but decided to wear a flannel shirt over my T-shirt instead. In the pack's front pocket was my red plastic bag of emergency supplies. I had no idea what was in that, it had been so long since I'd been on a major hike, but it was nearly six p.m. and I was already hungry, so I added a small bag of trail mix left over from Bob's recent solo backpack, and we headed off toward the top of our dirt road.

The road dead-ends at a semi-abandoned farm about a mile from our house. A local man who'd done some work for us the week before had talked about his childhood visits to the farm, and recalled a pond the original owner had dug up there sometime around 1910, to tan hide for snowshoes. Though we'd wandered the farmstead many times and never seen a hint of a pond, I wondered if it might still exist. I wanted to try to find it.

You couldn't drive to the farm even in a jeep, and in mud or snow or heat it was a wearing trek up the hill. But with only two modest dwellings apart from ours clustered in the valley near the stream, and a rarely used hunting camp about a quarter mile up the road, it was a pretty walk, through country once inhabited but long gone wild, haunted by ghostly corners of crumbled foundations and old stone walls. Just before the top, the road veered north and the landscape changed. There was a leveling of the forest floor, a hush as you entered a stand of tall white pines on a fragrant carpet of needles. The old white farmhouse appeared between the trees, alone in a large silence.

First glimpsed through a mist of pine needles, the house present-ed a fleeting impression of tidy white walls, set off by the elegant masonry of a stone chimney and foundation. It was only after coming into the clearing and getting much closer that one saw the many miss-ing window panes with plastic stapled to their frames, the scar above the door that marked a porch roof long gone. Evidence of time, age, neglect, was everywhere. And so was evidence of care.

Look closer still, and the structure seemed to stand by virtue of something short of a miracle; the next good gust could pummel it to a heap of boards and stones. Yet the clearing was mowed. A small cotton rug hung on a clothesline strung between two trees. A neat stack of firewood stood ready by the door. In front of the house, at the edge of the woods, a covered nineteenth-century well, its sides carefully screened from the elements, invited wishes.

Each time we visited, we'd scout the perimeter of the house to reassure ourselves that it was still intact, then continue on a mowed path to the barn and into the woods beyond, but we'd never gone far before the farm's mysteries grew deep, obscured by brambles and more or less, depending on the season, uninviting. This time, we walked a little further than we had before, then turned back and explored a path that took us through an old apple orchard and past a spring where I thought the pond would be, until tangled brush pressed us back. No pond.

"What now?" Bob asked.

We'd been walking only half an hour, and the late day light was so pleasant, it seemed too soon to go home.

Bob suggested we climb to a lookout point we called the ledges, half a mile beyond the farm. I was too lazy to make the climb without the reward of a sunset, and the sky was milky. "Why don't we take the ledges path," I suggested, "but instead of bushwhacking up the hill we could continue on the trail a little way, just to see where it goes."

From the mowed yard of the farmhouse, we entered the woods on a pine needle path from which it seemed every twig had been swept clean. The delight of walking on pine needles, apart from their fragrance, is that they render travel soundless, and out of this effortless silence rises something akin to reverence, which in turn inspires one to step even more softly, as if into a great cathedral. The silence becomes a presence, a deeply trusted companion. On such a clear, gentle path, it doesn't occur to one to turn back unless insects attack or obstacles appear, and perhaps not even then, because somewhere inside lurk notions of all kinds of possibility—notions? perhaps wishes?—that such a path could lead to another dimension, a magical realm, an ancestral home ancient beyond remembering.

We walked on until the old white pines gave way to mixed hard-woods and the clear trail underfoot disappeared into undifferentiated forest floor, its carpet the whitish brown of dead beech leaves as far as the eye could see, uneven, rolling, apparently pathless. Tags of red plastic ribbon, wrapped around tree trunks or tied to branches, now marked an informal trail: a property line, or a hunter's path.

The red tags led us gently uphill. Suddenly, or so it seemed, we were in a grove of old growth birch and beech trees—spare, straight, huge, a rare sight in these parts, where landowners sell their trees for profit or survival, and even the oldest parcels to come into the hands of the state have been logged within the last hundred years. It was far longer since there'd been logging here.

It's hard to say how far we'd traveled when the red tags stopped. At that moment, when we didn't turn back, but decided to go on from that place, we were lost.

But we didn't know it yet.

In addition to the tagged trees, we'd been noticing cairns, piles of stones often only a few yards apart, that someone had once laid to mark the way to somewhere. Now, though we could no longer find tags, the cairns continued, and I wanted to follow them.

We were careful. One of us stayed back in order to keep the last red tag in view, while the other walked on a little way, following cairns and trying to find another marker on a tree.

"We ought to turn back," Bob said.

"I know," I replied. "If we lose the property line we'll never get out of here." But I didn't want to turn back. The trees were so beautiful, the walking so gentle. Bob stayed back. I went off again. Found more cairns. In several directions. They must lead somewhere, I thought. But the urge to follow them didn't come from my mind. My body wanted to keep walking. What difference my body could discern between moving forward or going back the way we came, I have no idea. But forward was clearly where it wanted to go.

Many years ago, a friend told me about a phenomenon she called "the endless walk." The term had been used to describe the separate disappearances of several hikers in California. They vanished, it was said, not as a result of getting lost per se, but because of an inability to stop walking—or a compulsion to continue—rising perhaps from a pleasurable state in which endorphins flood the brain, overcoming reason, hunger, exhaustion, leading the oblivious to oblivion. An endless walk starts in pastoral innocence: a lighthearted outing with companions on a beautiful day, perhaps with a picnic as its centerpiece. The group pauses for a meal and a rest; a lone walker wanders on, mumbling something like, "I'm just going to see what's over here," then takes off—perhaps following a flash of color that intimates something beautiful or strange or familiar—and is never seen again. Having vaporized in a halo of gold light? Having perished in a field paved with chalky bones? Having achieved perfect union with the forest?

The long midsummer twilight was fading. I asked Bob what time it was. I tend to lose watches and am often without one. Bob wears his faithfully. But after swimming that afternoon, he'd left his watch on the dresser. Neither of us could guess the time. Prudently, we turned in the direction we'd come from—or thought we did—and looked for the red tag we'd been trying to stay near. Somehow we'd lost it. We made a slow, deliberate, tight circle around the clump of beech trees from which we'd set off through the cairns. We had no flashlight, no food to speak of, no water, no warm clothing. It was definitely time to head back.

Finally, perhaps a dozen yards away, we saw a faded, skinny strip of red plastic tied to a tiny twig. Good. And beyond it, I could see another tag. We began walking. Over some distance, we found perhaps half a dozen more blazes, scrambled over or around a few blowdowns we both thought were familiar, and then we noticed a pair of large pointy boulders, seven or eight feet high, sticking up side by side: a single rock long ago split in two. Neither of us could remember seeing this before. Ahead now, the next blaze, if there was one, eluded us. Nothing looked familiar. Apart from the twin boulders, nothing seemed especially unfamiliar either. We looked upward for a clue, but the light was too uniform, and the sky too obscured by great lush treetops to judge direction by its brightness. Again, we took turns, one staying back while the other struck out in this direction or that, hoping the pale, well-trodden leaves underfoot would reveal a path.

At least three times, we backtracked together to the first blaze—and each time returned to the same impasse of uncertainty. Could these be different red tags than the ones we'd followed to get here?

Once we'd posed this question, we knew we were lost.

I felt my heartbeat quicken, but thought, "This is ridiculous. How far could we be from the farmhouse? Two miles? Probably less."

I would have been happy enough just to press forward now by feel, following my sense of what looked familiar or felt right, which is more or less the way I move through life. But I had to admit this can be a dangerous impulse in the woods at dusk. I suggested a direction. Bob read the compass. "That can't be right," he said.

I thought of the red leaf. Somewhere very early on our trail, when we still knew exactly where we were, I had picked up a small fallen maple leaf, red and shiny, spotted with yellow and pale green and a darker green anyone would call blue if it hadn't been on a leaf. The perfect autumn leaf on August 3. I'd twirled it by its slender stem as I walked through the woods, and after a while I'd imagined dropping it, imagined someone finding it, some Sherlock or Watson who'd note that there were no maple trees in sight and deduce our passage from this single red leaf in the wrong place. It was the first red leaf I'd seen this year in the Adirondacks, where autumn starts to show when summer's barely in bloom. After carrying it for a long time, I'd let the leaf drift from my hand, half deliberately (thinking of Hansel and Gretel dropping bread crumbs first and pebbles when they knew better), somewhere back in the pines, on a narrow piece of trail where a bit of water rilled over some small rocks. An easily recognizable spot on this otherwise dry forest floor. Now in my mind's eye, I saw the red leaf where I'd dropped it, vivid even in the fading light, and assured myself that if we came to that place, I'd see the leaf and be certain we were going the right way. But I've never again seen that spot where the red leaf has long ago disappeared into the black earth.

Though it was still far from dark, we were finding it hard to see blazes from any distance. And whatever individual and joint certainties we had about where we were and what we saw (and where we'd just been and what we'd seen) were slipping. Was this really the same blowdown we'd just climbed over? Did it have that big crack? That layer of moss? That bluish fungus? Possibly. Maybe not. Since we were both normally attuned to such details, we became acutely aware that we were losing the security of our own perceptions. What had moments ago seemed as sure as our names, we now doubted.

I broke out the trail mix, hoping a little fuel would clear our heads. Nibbling a few peanuts and raisins and M&M's, we shuffled more or less in place through the leaves and studied the increasingly featureless trees. Bob took compass readings—to my shame, I'd never bothered to learn how—while I did my best to think things through. Back in our cabin, I'd absurdly roamed from room to room—how many times?—looking for my eyeglasses. Had I had them at hand, I now speculated uselessly, wouldn't ten more minutes of better light have had us back at the farm by now?

On the other hand, I could comfortably imagine spending the night right where we were in this lovely forest. I'd been keeping my eye out for any sort of rocky overhang or small cave that might provide some shelter, and I hadn't seen anything like that. Still, we had our trusty space blankets. I suggested to Bob that we just stop for the night here in the beech grove.

"No," he replied. "We'll get home." I could tell then from his voice that he was too agitated to pause and think, much less decide to settle now on a night in the woods. He behaved, however, as if he were unperturbed, turning this way, then that, studying the compass that lay like a pocket watch in his open palm.

From the pinpoint circle where we stood among the ivory leaves somewhere high in an old wood, all axes radiated to some unseen circumference. All we really knew was that we'd come uphill quite a way and had to go down. The farmhouse, I kept thinking. The farm. If we set off straight away on the right track, we had enough light to get back to the farm. From there we could easily get home in the dark. But Bob had another possibility in mind: a road.

Despite our bumbling in getting ourselves to this spot, we weren't completely unfamiliar with the general lay of the land, and we knew there was a paved road not very far to the southwest of the farm. Bob judged us to be much closer to this road now than we were to the farm. It was on this basis that he chose one of the 360 axes radiating from our point. "This is a path," he said. "It goes downhill. Follow me."

2

Follow me. I'd heard these words before. And though Bob usually did know where he was going, they often evoked doubt.

But follow him I did. If you've formed a picture of us strolling hand in hand through the forest like children or young lovers, erase it. That we never did, even at the very beginning. Most mountain trails are single-file affairs, and even on flat land I was usually slower than Bob. We tried, not always with success, to grant each other an individual pace. When this was working well, after an hour or so, I'd feel pleasantly mesmerized by the figure of the quick, tawny-haired man ahead of me, often wearing blue—work shirt, backpack, jeans—who seemed as if he were about to disappear into the sea of ferns that fluttered about his thighs.

On hot afternoons, certain ferns give off a luxuriant smell that reminds me of peach pie fresh from the oven. I've read that ferns once were believed to produce blue flowers that could be seen only at night —perhaps on only one night of the year—and only by people with special powers. I never saw one, but kept looking. These flowers are reputed to release invisible seeds that have the power of enchantment. Anyone able to gather the seeds (but how to do this?) could choose to make herself invisible or, if she preferred, she could scatter the seeds on the ground so that the earth's crust would become transparent, revealing treasure buried in its depths. In a half-dream, musing over the magical seeds and the blue flowers, I felt at times that I could walk behind Bob forever, nourished by the smell of imaginary peaches I could almost taste.

Other times, I wanted to kill him.

Bob didn't always know where he was going, even when he managed to persuade me that he did. In our early years, he'd routinely pushed me to climb mountains that proved more challenging than

I could comfortably manage. We'd read all we could find about a trail, I'd say, "I can't do that," to which Bob would reply, "Oh, come on. You can do it. It's no big deal. You'll love it." Sometimes I did love it, but when I hated it, I'd end up furious at both of us, mostly at myself for not following my own instincts. But at least half a dozen times I was convinced that what I had to do to get myself out of the place we'd gotten ourselves into would surely kill me, and I promised myself that, in the unlikely event that I returned to civilization alive, I would demand that Bob drive me to the nearest bus station, from whence I would get home on my own, never to see him again. But ultimately, I couldn't blame him when I'd freely taken on whatever adventure had proved so harrowing.

Throughout my childhood, nothing had been more thoroughly ingrained in me than avoiding physical danger. When I met Bob, however, I *wanted* to be the person who could haul a 40-pound pack around the woods for a week, scale sheer walls of rock, walk the knife edges. I'd had trouble with balance all my life, thanks to a congenital neck problem that had been surgically corrected when I was eight years old. At that point, when my parents should have made sure I learned to bike and skate and swim, they instead added violin lessons to the voice lessons I was already taking, setting me on a practice schedule that virtually confined me indoors. As an adult, however, after studying yoga for years, becoming a runner in my thirties and then a hiker, I'd finally known the exhilaration of some physical competence, and I wanted to take on the world. Then I discovered that the sight of water running over a rocky trail made my heart pound, that I was terrified of narrow edges and ledges. My legs shake uncontrollably when I attempt to rock-hop across the rushing steams Bob navigates like a gazelle. I have trouble crossing footbridges that have no handholds, and even some that do if they are very high or if they sway.

"Fear is your worst enemy," Bob would say. "You have to trust the mountain. Think of it as your friend."

But telling myself not to fear what I feared didn't work, and neither did doing what I feared and discovering that nothing terrible transpired. As for trusting mountains, I liked that idea, but it proved much easier for Bob to make friends with any random mountain than it was for me.

"But you did it, didn't you? Aren't you proud of yourself? Don't you feel good?" Bob would say kindly after some hair-raising trek during which I'd complained enough to try anyone's patience to the limit.

Sure, I was proud that I'd climbed Mt. Washington, the highest mountain east of the Mississippi, trudging past all the white crosses marking spots where less fortunate hikers had met their end. But I didn't enjoy being so scared. And when I'm scared, I'm no fun at all.

In spite of this, when I first began encouraging Bob to find other partners for the toughest treks, he insisted he wanted to do them with me. ("I hope you're not jealous," he said with trepidation the first time he confessed to doing a solo hike one weekend when I was out of town.) Eventually, though, he saw the wisdom in leaving me behind sometimes, and my brother became Bob's hiking partner for more rigorous ascents. This didn't mean I never found myself on a trail I wished I'd never started.

But here I was, nearly ten years later, still following Bob. Sometimes happily, sometimes reluctantly. Still in the woods.

It wasn't really a path we were on, but the dry bed of a streamlet. I didn't like it because it wasn't the way we'd come. It wouldn't take us to the farm. Whether it would take us out of the woods, I had no idea. But I had nothing better to offer apart from pure instinct, and so I followed.

Eventually the compass brought us to a place from which we could, as Bob had hoped, see western light, and then, not very far away, or at least so it seemed, a mountaintop, a long, flat-looking ridge, actually, against the sky. Bob thought he recognized this ridge and said he was sure that if we just kept to our southerly course, we'd come to a road. I was unconvinced, but the occasional distant rumble of a moving truck strengthened his case. The road sounds grew louder as we walked on, but no road appeared. Instead, the ground underfoot became wet, then almost impassable.

Unlike the serene but apparently pathless forest we'd left, this place was a labyrinthine confusion of ways. Roads and paths branched, turned corners, dead-ended in brush piles and brambles. It could have been days or years since loggers had slashed these passageways. Everything seeped with wetness. Though the mud seemed fresh, the wounds from this kind of logging go deep; recovery is long. Nonetheless, one or more of these roads certainly led out—or once had—carrying the trucks that hauled the logs to market. But if there were clues that might have told us which road met the outside world, we didn't know what to look for. And how far was the blacktop on which those logs were eventually transported, on which we could hitch a ride home? I had to agree with Bob that it was a wiser choice to follow the compass, even though that soon led us off these dubious tracks and back into the bush. Bob was unconcerned as long as we continued to head west. We just had to keep pressing ahead, he said, and we'd be out while we could still see daylight. I didn't believe it for a minute.

The scope of Bob's knowledge is prodigious. He can tell you how to tell a spruce from a fir, what minerals are found in most rocks, the age of any mountain range in the northern hemisphere, where in the night sky to look for any galaxy or nebula you care to name and at what season, the name of the largest of the amoebas (*Chaos chaos*), what's happening on the sun at any given time, and he probably knows even more about music than he does about the physical world.

But self-doubt is his nemesis, and common sense is not a common thing for him to summon up. Some illogical kink in the way he figures things often thwarts him. Some people, when faced with a mechanical dilemma, find practical shortcuts in a flash. My brother and my daughter are like this. Bob is the opposite: he tends to add unnecessary steps to things or skip essential ones. In the face of frustration or uncertainty, he often succumbs to a fugue of ineptness, becoming too impatient with what he's doing to follow through, insisting all the while that he will succeed, while thwarting himself at every turn by refusing to stop and think. This of course confirms his general expectation that things will go wrong. There are two areas, however, in which his optimism is predictably excessive: the weather, and how far we are from any given destination, on foot or in the car.

After the fact, he'll often admit that overabundant enthusiasm and pigheaded certainty that he's heading in the right direction have contributed to his becoming confused and going the wrong way. At such times, he'll stonewall me, refuse to hear my point of view rather than consider the possibility that he might be mistaken. I suspected this was one of those times.

We were knee-deep in ferns now, fallen trees concealed by the ferns, black mud and wetter muck in which the ferns were growing. Though I guessed it was no more than twenty minutes since we'd come down the hill, I knew I couldn't find my way back up the way we came. I tried not to think about this. If Bob was right it wouldn't matter. But I didn't think he was right, and I was as disturbed by the unfamiliarity of this terrain as I was by its difficulty. We could be anywhere at all. Above, lost on the hill, the farmhouse in my mind's eye had nonetheless anchored me. Here, I felt adrift in a featureless sea.

I was certain we wouldn't get out of the woods tonight, and I only wanted a dry place to stop. Bob, expecting to see our mythic exit around every bend, and more uneasy than I about a night outside, was determined to push forward. As we did, we broke several cardinal rules of backcountry travel, to compound those we'd started breaking the minute we walked out of the cabin with virtually nothing but our pocket knives and the clothes on our backs. The *Boy Scout Handbook* would have urged us to stay put in the beech forest until morning. But not only had we continued walking for perhaps an hour without a clue about where we were going—we'd now stopped relying strictly on the compass as well. It was simply too difficult. Every path soon forked into at least two oblique and impassible choices. Some dissolved into dense woods, others became so muddy and overgrown we had to backtrack. Whenever we came to something open and dry enough to walk on, we went that way. Our movements had become a series of random forays down blind alleys.

I was having difficulty keeping up with Bob. The dimmer the light, the faster he moved and the less sure my footing. And I was tiring. In my haste I kept tripping over slimy logs camouflaged by ferns. I fell several times. Finally I insisted we stop.

We found a small piece of dry land, a little hummock that stood a few feet above the logging debris, with a clearing large enough for us to stretch out. Without a word, as if we'd done this hundreds of times before, we took up tasks: I set about collecting firewood. Bob began gathering big branches to construct a shelter as night closed off the forest around us.

Decades earlier, when I was seven months pregnant, I moved from Manhattan with my husband to a place we thought of as the country. We'd taken a cheap winter rental, a big, drafty, sparsely furnished house on three acres in East Hampton, Long Island, now known for celebrities and traffic jams. I was a young writer, my husband was a music student, and apart from a Steinway upright, we owned almost nothing. Among the few things we brought to furnish our new lives, there was only one that had no specific function: a large wicker market basket I'd inherited from my grandmother. But as soon as I got to the country I knew exactly what to do with it. An hour after we'd arrived, as evening fell, I went alone into a briar-laced wood I hadn't yet explored in daylight, and with the basket's sturdy handle resting on my arm, wandered off to gather firewood.

It was the first time I had ever done this simple thing, but there was an eerie familiarity to it: walking through a wooded place, seeking and finding in dark corners, filling a basket. And on this August night, decades later, once more in an unfamiliar forest, I filled my arms with sticks and twigs and felt a strange sense of homecoming.

Carefully, in the last pale moment of dusk, I laid the fire. I looked up to see a ruby-throated hummingbird whizzing toward my red flannel shirt; discovering that I was no flower, he swiftly arced away. The first time I saw hummingbirds I was sitting alone on a rock on a mountainside while Bob explored a nearby cave. I heard a loud buzzing, looked for an insect, and saw three dragonflies that turned into miraculous hummingbirds as my eyes adjusted to their newness and allowed the birds to assume their own shape. I'd vowed to spend more time sitting still in the wild, still and alone, in order to see what would reveal itself. *Have I done that?* I thought. *No, I have not. But I can do it right now.*

When I had a small fire going I sat on the ground and rested my back against the trunk of a hemlock tree. I felt completely relaxed. In fact, lost in the darkness, without supper, shelter, flashlight, or water, some part of me was rejoicing. I was a bit tired, but not yet hungry or thirsty or cold. And we were in the woods. I love the woods. I trust the woods. And it occurred to me that somehow I had acquired a house when what I really wanted—probably what we'd both really wanted—was simply to live outdoors. Of course, in this climate, that wasn't quite possible. But for the moment, now that we had stopped walking for the night, and before I would allow myself to think about tomorrow, I was so delighted to be facing a night without walls, I was perfectly happy to be lost.

I knew that without food or water or sleep, the clarity of mind I had, the energy I felt, would leave me, unreal and impossible as that seemed. There was a small handful of trail mix left for each of us. I opened my emergency kit. It contained bandaids, antiseptic, matches, rope, and whistles, but nothing to eat apart from four coffee-to-go packets of white sugar. The only water we'd seen was in mudholes. Disordered thinking, surely our greatest threat, seemed inevitable. At least we could stave it off as long as possible by avoiding anything that would encourage it, like catastrophizing or panicking. I got up and went to hunt more wood.

A gritty scream shredded the night. It was not quite pitch black beyond our little hummock. Bob and I, busy at our respective tasks had our backs to each other and the small fire that sputtered between us. I froze and listened. Bobcat, I thought. "Bobcat," he said. His voice, straining to sound calm, told me he was terrified.

Bob is brave, if not foolhardy, about physical risks. In New Hampshire's White Mountains he insisted we proceed with a back-packing trip despite thunder and lightning. In New Mexico's Gila Wilderness, he climbed a rattlesnake-infested mesa and disappeared for an hour in the midday sun while the rest of our group sat at the edge of heat stroke in a desolate canyon, immobilized by fatigue. But he's actually afraid of a lot of things that don't scare me. And whatever made that unearthly sound was one of them.

Seconds later, the scream was followed by a familiar, rhythmic call. We realized both sounds had been produced by the same angry creature: a barred owl. The bird was very near, and upset by our presence. Perhaps the hemlock that sheltered us was its favorite hunt-ing outpost or its roost. In less ominous tones, solitary, never coming closer, it kept us company.

Probably at least a dozen kinds of carnivorous mammals roam these woods and bobcats are among the nastiest, but if they've ever attacked humans in the northeast, I haven't heard of it. I knew there was little chance of danger from wild animals, and of course Bob knew that, too. Black bears are the only potential threat to people who are minding their own business. And I wasn't worried about bears. Since we had no food, there was no reason for them to be drawn to us. Perfume and other cosmetic smells may anger bears, but a bear who picks up natural human scent from a distance typically runs the other way. Nor had I seen anything in the terrain we'd been through that bears like to eat: nuts, acorns, berries. It's possible you could cross the path of a bear just about anywhere in the forest. But given that the Adirondacks is home to about five thousand bears in six million acres, the odds are against it.

Bob's fear, however, was less specific. It didn't necessarily involve real animals at all. I'd learned this when we'd known each other about a year.

We'd been hiking in a small state park not far from Manhattan one Saturday in June, and when evening drew near, I didn't want to go home. Some rudimentary camping equipment we'd recently acquired was in Bob's car, and even though there were no camping areas in this particular preserve, I persuaded Bob to spend the night out.

We bushwhacked into the woods a few hundred yards from the car, staked our tent while it was still light, then drove off to a general store in a nearby town, where we bought the best they had: a package of franks, a can of beans, a jar of instant coffee and a loaf of bread.

After dinner, we sat on the ground talking in front of a discreet fire. Though the day had been stunningly clear, the night was overcast and windy. Bob was clearly feeling a little nervous, and he was talking about going to check on the car when I put out my hand to hush him. I'd heard a sound. Twigs breaking. Turning, I saw a dim shape, perhaps five yards away, blacker than the black trees against the dark sky.

"There's something over there," I said quietly. "There is a large animal right over there." It was too large to be anything but a bear.

"Where's the flashlight?"

His voice was tremulous, and I knew right away he was more afraid than I was. I found the flashlight on the ground next to my knee, and I was about to hand it, unlit, to him, but instead I pointed it in the direction of the dark shape and flicked it on. In its yellow circle of light we saw, large and round, a buttonbush, its short branches motionless in the windy night.

When we'd stopped laughing, I asked, "What would we have done if it was a bear?"

"Run like hell."

"Not from bears. You run from snakes, not bears. Bang pots," I remembered reading. "That's what you do."

"How about bang pots from inside the tent," Bob asked, uncurling himself from the ground.

"Fine. But we only have one pot." I hit it with my hand, producing a dull thump unlikely to frighten anything.

Nonetheless, we zipped ourselves into the tent and sat cross-legged, facing each other with the foolish little cooking pot between us.

"I don't know about you," Bob said, "but I don't feel much like taking off my clothes."

"It's a little cold."

"Not just that. Somehow, it doesn't seem like a good idea."

"'Fraid of the dark?" I teased. Bob had exceptionally sharp night vision. When he set up his telescope, he frequently complained that the sky wasn't dark enough, and even when clouds obscured the heavens, he preferred to walk about without a flashlight.

"Not the dark," he replied unconvincingly. "Okay, the dark is part of it. If there was a moon, even a sliver of a moon—but it's really dark. And no stars. It's like losing one of your senses."

I estimated that the darkness would last about six more hours, which didn't seem so terribly long to me.

"Six more hours!" Bob groaned. "Just listen to all that stuff going on out there. All my life, I've been so acutely attuned to sound and right now it's just overwhelming."

I heard wind whooshing through trees. Somewhere nearby, a creek gurgled.

"In the city, you have to shut out all the sounds," Bob went on. "You can't possibly pay attention to them all, or identify all of them, and mostly they don't have anything to do with you anyway, but in the woods, anything you hear could affect you."

I took off my boots. Bob removed his. Twigs and bushes rustled. Light footsteps, a mouse or a vole, came near and passed. We crawled between the two open sleeping bags. My hands were cold, but otherwise I felt warm enough. Bob was shivering. I slipped my hand inside his shirt.

"Are you still terrified?"

"I don't know what's out there. I feel...vulnerable."

"What scares you?"

"I don't know. The creatures of the night, I guess."

Monsters, I thought. They are not out *there*. Under my hand I felt the trepidations of Bob's heart, and I wondered if what frightened him in the loud night was not the forest's huge and complex otherness, but some wildness in himself.

The shelter Bob built was like a nest: boughs and branches piled against a big stump, roughly interwoven and covered with heaps of leaves. It would have been perfect for one or two very slim people about three and half feet tall. We are both of average size. Nonetheless, though it was only wide enough, and not long enough, for one of us to lie flat, it definitely counted as sleeping quarters. And regardless of rain or nest, what I'd been counting on for an acceptably comfortable night were the two mylar space blankets that had accompanied me on every hike I'd taken in the last ten years. Their time had come. I tore open one of the worn cellophane wrappers and with chilled, clumsy fingers attempted to unfold the "blanket." The mylar stuck together. Gently, I tried to separate the folds. I pulled a little harder. The stuff shredded. Bob tried the other, with the same result. At some point in that decade of presumed readiness our security blankets had disintegrated.

It was astonishing, when we lay down, how cold it was.

We'd managed to unravel enough mylar to line the bottom of the nest and break the coldness of the ground a little if we both lay on our sides against each other, with as little body surface as possible resting on the ground. We took turns shivering, depending on who had the warmer position, near the back wall of the shelter.

When I was five years old, I sang in the chorus of Humperdinck's "Hansel and Gretel." My mother's sister, who ran a music school where I was soon to begin a decade of vocal study, mounted a production of the opera each Christmas at Philadelphia's Town Hall. By the time I was permitted on stage, I'd sat in the audience for several seasons of performances and rehearsals, and had committed to memory every word of the libretto. As a small child, I learned a great many lyrics in half a dozen languages, and to this day still have snatches and fragments of the most unlikely and irrelevant stuff knocking about in my head. The few words that had stayed with me from the Humperdinck opera were sung when night fell upon the lost children. The stage lights dimmed; the hapless pair huddled together under a tree; the chorus sang...."Now I lay me down to sleep/Fourteen angels round my feet/Two are at my right hand/Two are at my left hand...." How were the other ten angels distributed? What were the rest of the words?

Was I three when the story was first read to me from a Little Golden Book? Two? Is that why I found myself on this midsummer's night huddled against a pile of sticks on the cold ground, instead of in the Hamptons where, in my late thirties, I left a relatively comfortable though tumultuous life with a man who liked living near the woods but did not want to encounter them? Was it because of that long ago chorus in which I lifted my small voice to sing of guardian angels that, half a lifetime later, I felt no fear in the middle of the night in the dark woods, even though my male companion did?

Hours ago, I'd zipped myself into my hooded windbreaker, and though the thin nylon fabric was unlined, indeed, almost transparent, it cut a little of the cold. From time to time, Bob and I both got up, refueled the fire, sat by it and got warm, then sleepy, then lay down again. When we bumped the shelter's walls or roof from inside, which we managed to do whenever we shifted position, dirt fell through the branches, and I thought of Edgar Allen Poe's tales, and about being alive in a grave with bits of earth falling on my head.

We knew we needed a plan, logic, a way to avoid wasting energy by wandering pointlessly in the morning. I confessed that I couldn't retrace our path back up the hill and Bob admitted he probably couldn't either, at least not more than part way. I was dubious about continuing in the direction we'd been taking. And I verbalized something else I'd known all along, but had been afraid to say: If the road we heard was the road we thought it was, a stream lay between us and it. Though it was a road we traveled often, the stream was far back, at no point visible, and we had no idea how wide or deep it was, or how the land lay at its banks. Bob was counting on our being able to cross the stream. I reminded him I couldn't swim. There would be no boatman waiting, as there was in so many myths and stories, to take us across. I envisioned us finally coming to the road only to find it beyond water, out of reach.

In the night, we discussed the possibilities briefly once or twice but reached no decision about what we would do at daybreak.

Distant lightning sheared the sky. No thunder. We heard planes, an occasional truck on a road not far away, no woods sounds. I wondered if the hiker who'd died two summers ago near Lewey Lake had heard the road that lay three miles from the campsite where he'd perished from exposure.

I know I slept because, waking, I knew I had dreamed, though I couldn't say what.

I opened my eyes and saw sky that was lighter than the trees. It was like a photograph gone from negative to positive, for in the darkest part of the night, against the glowing coals of the fire, the trees gave off a little light. When I stood up, the oncoming day seemed like an illusion. All seemed equally black above. Bob got up, too. Don't think about coffee, I told myself. Not a passing thought. We revived the fire. A wood thrush began to sing a long and complicated song. The sky turned indigo.

The night was over. It hadn't rained. We were still lost.

PART II

Vanishing Points

Stand still. The trees ahead and bushes beside you
Are not lost. Wherever you are is called Here
…Stand still. The forest knows
Where you are. You must let it find you.

"Lost", David Wagoner

3

In the night, we'd agreed on a plan to head back uphill, to follow the compass faithfully, to head west. But as the sky paled enough to enable us to see beyond the cold remains of our fire, we faced a universe of possibility we hadn't apprehended in the dark. We'd camped at a confluence of roads cut by loggers. The hope that one of these roads would quickly lead us out was irresistible.

Up above, we could visualize nothing but pathless forest; in comparison, anything the imagination could construe as a route used by mammals—all the more, a stretch of road that had once seen motorized travel!—offered temptation. We reasoned, as Bob had at dusk, that if we followed some road to its conclusion, we'd find our way back to civilization faster than trekking through the bush.

But this was not necessarily true, I reminded myself. Not on a logging road. We'd hit enough dead ends in the woods over the years to understand that the logic of getting trees out of the forest bears little relation to that of human foot travel. Every road has a story to tell, with a beginning, a middle and an end, and if somewhere along the way you can decipher that story, you will know where you are. Logging, too, has its story, but it was in a language we hadn't taken the trouble to learn when we taught ourselves to read the Adirondack landscape. We both knew more about the geological bubbling and cooling that had taken place here more than a billion years ago than we did about the way this land had been reshaped over the last few centuries by the industry of harvesting trees.

Now, in the perplexing dawn, we walked tentatively along a wide path lined with shoulder-high shrubs. The footing was firm, the walking easy; for a moment, I imagined there could be houses nearby. But something was not right: too many quick turns and crisscrossing paths. The uniform height of the vegetation suggested a clearcut perhaps ten years old. Each bend we rounded revealed more of the same. Before long, I suspected we were walking in circles. Logging roads are rarely through roads. More often than not, miles or yards from the start, they loop around on themselves or simply stop. If they're in good condition, as these were, neither sandy nor muddy nor rutted, they encourage the nimble to cover more ground in less time which, if you happen to be going the wrong way, enables you to get more lost more quickly. The one virtue of such roads is this: if you haven't taken too many turns or byways, they make it relatively easy to backtrack and start over. Within moments, that's what we did.

Returning to our campsite, we approached it from a slight rise this time, and as I looked down on the hummock where we'd spent the night I was surprised at how small it seemed in the pale light, and how insignificant, like nothing really, in the expanse before us. It hadn't become, in the way a campsite typically does for the time one claims it, a "real" place, a home. Even primitive backcountry sites, with no picnic table, no fireplace, nor even a ring of stones around a bit of charred earth—even those flicker back and forth across a shady curtain in perception, one moment differentiated, a unique locus in the universe, the next, no place at all. And it made me uneasy to realize, though it's obvious, that we impose on the backcountry campsite an identity we snuff out when we pull our tent stakes; when we move on, it is absorbed back into the forest, an anonymous square of earth in the unmapped territory of dream.

What would it be like, I wondered, to start a life in such a place, from nothing, after a long journey on foot or by wagon? Not like this. We'd have possessions, I thought, at least a few pots and pans, a blanket, some sort of food and a plan for getting more, maybe even tools. And an idea.

Today, there were no stakes to pull, no pots to pack, no sleeping bags to roll. The time, we guessed, was no more than 4:30 or 5 when we carefully kicked dirt over the faint remains of our fire and set out to find our way home.

Though we are meticulously clean campers, much tidier than we are indoors, we decided without speaking of it not to dismantle our curious shelter with its shredded mylar floor. It seemed prudent to leave some sign of our passage, even though it was likely no one else had passed here since last winter's deer season, if then, and the beginning of this year's was three months away. That we might be in the woods long enough for someone to come looking for us was unimaginable. And yet not strictly so. So we left the shelter and the mylar in the spirit of a young, healthy person preparing a last will and testament: on one level, you know you're mortal, but on another you remain unconvinced.

The compass led us relatively quickly uphill over much better terrain than we'd slogged through at dusk. As we climbed, sunlight came filtering through the leaves, the scars of logging receded and the forest began to look cleaner. Beech trees! I felt a leap of hope, then doubt. Is this what I think it is? I kept asking myself.

It wasn't. The trees weren't nearly as large as those among which we'd lost ourselves. The terrain was, again, all new, a forest of mixed hardwoods, last logged, the size of the trees suggested, 30 or 40 years ago. It resembled nothing we'd seen last night. And today, I not only wanted the familiar, I expected it, unreasonably demanded it, mentally stomping my feet in a tantrum. Again came the thought: We could be anywhere. A cavern of fear opened in me.

We climbed on. Fear has momentarily paralyzed me more than once in the woods, as in my life. I'd find myself on some slick rock slide, lifting my foot, unable to see a place that looked safe to put it down, unable, I felt, to take one more step. In the last painfully stuck years of my marriage, I knew it could not go on as it was, and that I'd done everything I could to change it, yet I could not get myself to leave. You simply must do something, I finally told myself. Keep moving, the woods have told me. This is not necessarily the thing to do when confronted by a wild animal, something I'd never experienced and rarely thought to fear. But scrambling up boulders above tree line, crossing a slippery log bridge, rock-hopping in deep, fast water, *keep moving,* I order my terrified self. And even in the scariest places, simply moving, if it doesn't banish fear, usually blunts its edge.

We climbed on and before very long, high above us, we saw light through the treetops, something open ahead.

"I know this flat rock, don't you?" I exclaimed.

"It's the ledges. What else could it be?"

Ledges! We'd found the ledges after all on the drunken path we'd plotted up the hill. Now we broke with the compass and headed for the brightness.

Carefully observing the familiar boulders under our feet, we circumvented some prickly black spruce and scrambled up to a sun-bathed, precipitous viewpoint. By everything we could touch, we stood in a place where we'd stood many times. But these were not our ledges.

The mountain across the valley was different. It had a longer, flatter top than the one we knew. A white building nestled against its side. From our ledges, there was no structure to be seen. Though the blue-gray granitic gneiss under our feet, with all its complex creases and cracks, seemed familiar as the lined face of a beloved elder, we were on a strange ridge looking across a deep valley at another ridge we'd never seen before. That was all we knew. We were nowhere.

"How can this be? It's impossible." I felt my bearings falling away from me. My panic gushed forth in a stream of pointless words. "Now what? What do we do now?" I moaned, as if this were entirely Bob's fault, and I had nothing to do with getting us here.

"We go back to where we broke with the compass," Bob said calmly. "We pick up where we left off, and keep going from there."

"But where are we?" I demanded for the third or fourth time. "What's that ridge?"

"I don't know," Bob said patiently. "But when you're ready, I think we should move on."

He'd caught me on a downward slide and I righted myself. And we fell together into a shared rhythm: waves of intense feelings, shifting between anxiety and hopelessness to an almost objective absorption in the great puzzle of it all.

One of the first questions we were later asked about this time in the woods was whether we fought. It was asked not only by those who know that we are not always a harmonious couple, but also by others who, themselves by temperament less volatile than either of us, identified with that aspect of our situation that invited discord.

Bob's colleagues at school nicknamed him "Sparky," a name that just as easily could have been tagged on me for my flash-powder temper. Bob earned the epithet for the lightning he makes in his physics class with his Van de Graaff generator, plus the fact that he's always sparking holes in his shirts during chemistry experiments, and not least because of his combustible personality. On another level, it was meant with irony, because he is as often stolid and gloomy as he is lively, talkative and enthusiastic.

And here we were, in a perfect fix for bickering, blaming and recrimination. Whose fault was this pickle? It could be analyzed ad nauseum. Any of a dozen moments in the last twelve hours—or the last twelve years—could have been cited as the one that had set us on an inevitable course to this misadventure. In addition, either of us is by nature as likely to cope badly with frustration as to cope well, and at bickering, blaming, and sulking, we are adept. Probably we would have parted ways years ago were we not also adept at quick forgiveness.

This time, however, we avoided bickering and blame. Instead, in what some students of human dynamics would call a classic demonstration of the homeostasis of self-regulating systems, we took turns getting hysterical.

Balancing each other's states of mind like a pair on a see-saw, one up, one down, we somehow navigated the shoals of our emotions. What was most important about this see-saw act was that it meant the voice of reason, springing sometimes from my mouth, sometimes from his, at no moment altogether left us.

We retraced our steps through the hardwoods, and the compass led us to other ledges, again unfamiliar, and from there, back through more young forest and sharply down. My mind drifted toward the entrancement of the endless walk. I was following Bob through the woods as I'd followed him for so many years, so many miles, with trust, mistrust, it no longer mattered. I was pleasantly mesmerized by the sweet smells of the forest and the soft light filtering through summer leaves. So it seemed to me quite sudden, after the kind of abrupt yet seamless set change that occurs in dreams, that the landscape had gone from dry to wet. We were in bottomlands again, wilder and less disturbed by human intervention than those in which we'd found ourselves at dark last night, but equally mucky and problematic to traverse.

How did we get here? The transition to this new vista, steamy, green and dark as the jungle, seemed to occur both very quickly and with a great deal of effort. I awoke as if from true sleep to find myself trudging through a swale of waist-high ferns and slippery, rotten deadfall, half-buried in standing water or spongy moss—a fabulously rich microcosm of composition and decomposition, creation and decay. I surveyed the scene in confusion. Sharp rays of sun pierced the canopy to gild the arcing plumes of ostrich ferns that fluttered in a thicket all around me. The light pulsed in the almost imperceptible breeze and my mood shifted with it. I was reminded of a sultry afternoon when we'd traversed terrain like this near my brother's house in Paradox, some twenty miles from ours. I couldn't recall where we'd been trying to go, but only that it had been Bob's idea and how hot and difficult it had become, how angry I was to be stumbling after him through the muck—until I found a stand of blue vervain, a common weed but scarce in my experience. I remembered my happiness at being able to pick a few stalks, how graceful I found its candelabra shape in the vase where I eventually dried it, and that it remained beautiful to my eyes for years.

I thought again of the red leaf, somewhere, the farmhouse, somewhere, an equally tiny and remote anchor point in what only now—after at least twelve hours in the forest—struck me as wilderness. Like the pivotal moments we recognize as landmarks when we retrospectively map the vastness of our lives, these two images flashed now, the only clear, bright points in the dim scramble of the previous evening.

The land of wrong turns, I thought. *My life.* It's been the curse of my particular makeup to revisit more often than is wise or useful those points from which I map where I went wrong. I ask too often, *How did I get from there to here?* The asking may be no more insistent than the hum of an air conditioner. Sometimes, though, it is pressing, as if knowing the way I'd come, I could retrace my path through time, start over, be 22 when I decided against graduate school; 28 when, under contract for my second novel, I abandoned fiction to write television soaps; 34, when, after a two-year separation from my husband, I went back to try again. Sidetracked by conflicting jobs, ambitions, lovers, by migraine headaches, material desires, lust, unhappy love, I blamed wrong turns for the fact that I hadn't accomplished more as a writer. The most significant of these choices involved taking writing jobs for money, rather than struggling with art.

How? What, exactly, was my route? Each time, a different answer. Wasn't it there, where I abandoned the novel, that I went wrong? I uselessly ask, forgetting that at the time I had a two-year-old, and a husband who was suffering from a mysterious heart ailment, and that, when the soap job came up, I was supplementing the tiny advance I'd received for my novel by stuffing envelopes in a real estate office for below minimum wage. Could I have known that I would never find my way through that novel, that the editor who'd bought it would soon die, that my husband would regain his health, that this job would begin a digression through an entire decade? Daytime serial writing demands, among other things, an acute attentiveness to every nuance of the actor's voice. It left me struggling to relearn the rhythms of my own, asking *how did I get here?* I thought I was taking the right path. *How did I lose my way?*

The leaf, the farmhouse. Between there and here, I saw only a tangle.

And I felt these anchor points, like pieces of the past, continually receding. The smaller the pieces become over time's distance, the larger the risk of clinging to something no longer complete or correct, a story with crucial parts innocently forgotten, or significant details altered by the ever-vigilant subconscious. It is surely as often by reshaping the past as by imagining the future that we propel ourselves into the rest of our lives. Our minds are made to seek pattern. It is not a matter of choice that we fix meaning on chaos and superimpose the familiar on the strange.

The sun was high now, the morning hot.

Out of the confusion of the ferns and low shrubs of the seep, my eye picked out a distant stand of Scotch pine—an introduced tree, its coppery bark scaling in big slabs, evocative of ponderosa and the west —and balsam fir, a true native, the emblematic tree of the north woods. These are the significant trees that shade our end of the road, and it occurred to me I hadn't seen either species since well before we'd reached the farm last evening. Wouldn't they lead us to others of their kind?

I wanted to take them as my advance guard, to follow the senses that were pointing me straight ahead and with a slight tack to the right, toward those trees. Surely they would lead us home! Bob, who has taught me ninety-eight percent of what I know about trees, persuaded me this was wishful thinking.

Besides, the compass said we should be heading in the opposite direction, where we faced alder bushes and a break in the canopy. This meant we were near a stream. A stream or river is always a good thing to find when you're lost, or so we'd read in every orienteering book we'd ever cracked. In nine cases out of ten, I remembered one book saying, a river will lead to somebody's home, if not your own. More important, we'd been sweating profusely, with nothing to drink. We had to take advantage of any opportunity to drink water, even if that meant we'd come down with giardia or some other bug in a couple of weeks. I didn't actually feel thirsty, and, always tempted to go with instinct, I was reluctant to turn my back on the familiar conifers. But, yes, it was a good thing to be near a stream, and I was not going to insist on walking off, at the beckoning of some trees, in the opposite direction.

"Near," of course, is always a relative term. When used to describe the distance between streams and alder, all it really means is that there is, or was, in the geologically recent past, some sort of water (a lake, a swamp, an ancient inland sea, a puddle) within a mile beyond the thicket. Also possibly under it.

It is in the nature of an alder swamp (also known as a beaver meadow) to be almost impenetrable—though I always forget this until I venture into one. Alder in these parts are typically just a little taller than the average person. You can't see over them, you can't see between their dense, scratchy little gray branches and you can't see around the great clumps in which they tend to grow. In addition, dry or wet, the ground is usually covered with odds and ends the beavers left when they chomped through the trees, carrying off some branches and dining on others, and turned the place into a flood plain. But since you can't see the ground, you can't anticipate and adjust your

stride to this slippery old wood or to other obstacles like the occa-
sional rock at your feet. Walking in an alder swamp you simply can't
see where you're going. We could see only what was directly in front
of us: gray-branched shrubs, with small, leathery ovate leaves inches
from our eyes.

In the Ituri rain forest of northeastern Zaire, the Mbuti pygmies
spend their lives in such an undifferentiated landscape, "visually
unorganized," geographer Yi-Fu Tuan calls it, where anything that is
seen is seen at close range. One of the chief distinctions of this rain for-
est as human habitat is its all-enveloping nature. "It is not differentiat-
ed as to sky and earth," says Tuan, "there is no horizon; it lacks land-
marks." This has an interesting impact on what the Mbuti make of the
world. People in most other environments define life on earth as one of
several planes of existence, with heavens above and underworld below,
and either or both preceding and/or following our sojourn here. The
Mbuti cosmology lacks these strata; the forest is its only plane, and it
is the source of all things material and spiritual—reward and punish-
ment, food and shelter, the past, the future, and the hereafter. In the
forest the Mbuti place the profound trust usually reserved for deities.

The curtailment of perspective in the all-encompassing forest has
disadvantages more significant than the distortion of spatial percep-
tion. The inability to see at any distance carries a primal danger:
predators can't be seen until they're little more than a jaw's snap away.
At least partly in order to defend against such ambush, most humans
are believed to prefer to live in terrain that resembles park-like
savanna, or other environments with expansive views that mitigate
against surprise attack.

To me, however, the Mbuti's preferences and their perception of
their dark wood as nurturing and protective makes perfect emotional
sense. They mirror my own affinity for the forest's close embrace, a
yearning that, though it lay dormant for decades, has probably dwelt
in me most of my life.

The forests of my childhood were located between the covers of books, among the first of which was that slim volume entitled *Hansel and Gretel*. Later came *Little Red Riding Hood, Peter and the Wolf, Snow White*. I pictured the wild woods in which these tales were set as tight, fast universes, affording no broad vistas to warn of distant danger or hint at the world outside. The dwindling path common to the illustrations led only one way: ever deeper into the wild. It's hard to say why these forests held for me a reality far more vivid and personal than the Emerald City of Oz, Captain Hook's pirate ship, Cinderella's hearth, or any of the other storied places of my childhood. But perhaps it's because I somehow knew forests were real, that places like this did exist somewhere.

When fairy tales were read to me, and in all the years when I read and reread them myself, and later to my little brother, I'd never seen anything the slightest bit like a forest. Yet the very idea of it somehow liberated me from my mother's oppressive watchfulness: *Don't touch, don't run, don't yell, don't get dirty....* In the dark wood of my childish mind I could do any and all these things with impunity and, eventually, a great many other things as well.

In a dim place filled with moist, shiny leaves and succulent berries, there were forbidden corners, secrets, magic and adventure. Bog and fen, glade and swale alike hid sacred groves, pagan rites, and many things forgotten, buried, important. There were stories in every rock and tree if you knew how to read them. Light and shadow, smell and wind could tell hundreds of tales, too, as they must have to the storytellers who first wandered a wood and imagined frogs transformed to princes, sleeping beauties awakening, and spirits of every sort of inclination invisibly hovering among the adumbrating trees. The forest was, as Marina Warner says of fairy tales, a "huge theatre of possibility" where, as in fairy tales, anything can happen.

Some of these things are, of course, very very bad. Fairy tales are scary, and—I tend to forget this—a great many people regard the woods with terror. There, beyond the reach of all the protective—and suffocating—supports and prohibitions of family and society, one is profoundly vulnerable. Of course, I'd been taught I should feel vulnerable almost anywhere. The most definitive information my mother conveyed to me was that the world beyond the home is fraught with danger. Despite my awareness of her own romantic yearnings to partake of that world, her admonitions rendered me forever far more fearful than brave. Still, when I entered the woods, I almost always felt safe. That the forest was a place of danger, loneliness and banishment to the vagaries of wolves and witches had apparently impressed me far less than the transformative events that took place there. If you didn't like who you were, you could become someone else. And, as many students of fairy tales have noted, it was frequently an adventure in the forest that preceded "happily ever after."

So now here I was stuck in an alder meadow, and it evoked in me no feelings of security, no hope for happy endings, but something like rage. I wanted to beat at these skinny gray trees, tear at their tough branches to break through the claustrophobia of this labyrinthine, lid-less box. Wasn't it in this sort of place that Briar Rose went to sleep for a hundred years?

I was stumbling a lot, as I had at dusk. I wasn't sure if this was because my energy was flagging, or because I was tripping over things I couldn't see. Too dense and resilient to beat against, the alders demanded the most intimate of encounters. Tree by tree, step by step, we squeezed ourselves between the scratchy branches until, when at last we emerged into the light, it felt as if they'd sprung open and released us. We found ourselves on a bit of solid ground, dark with comforting old hemlocks. Scratched and trembling, I followed Bob to the edge and stood with him, finally, on a narrow bank about three feet above a placid stream. Its sunlit blue openness spread so sinuously we couldn't see very far upstream or down. Across the water, dense forest seemed to mirror the landscape in which we stood.

We'd hoped that once we could see a stream we wouldn't be lost anymore, for we were reasonably sure there were only two in the area: Alder Brook, which Bob thought we could follow out to a road, and Trout Brook, much of which Bob had explored by canoe, and which would lead us back to our house. It hadn't occurred to us that we might be unable to distinguish one from the other.

"Do you know where we are?" I asked Bob, expecting him to say yes. "I have no idea," he replied. "I've never seen this place before. But this water looks clean and I'm going to drink some. You should, too."

Backcountry travelers have always faced the risk that the purest looking water may be contaminated by animal waste. Since the late 70s, however, no water has been considered safe for drinking in the woods of the northeast, no matter how remote the location, because of the volume of human traffic through what remains of the wilderness. But of course Bob was right. We had to drink.

Among the whistles and the snakebite kit, the well-aged benadryl and the other worthless supplies in my pack was a clean plastic bag, which made an adequate drinking vessel. Though I should have felt thirsty, I still didn't. Actually, I felt sick to my stomach. I gave the bag to Bob and scurried into the underbrush. When I returned he was climbing back up the bank with the bag full of clear water. "Drink this," he said.

I hesitated. Preferring to conceal how lightheaded I felt, I was reluctant to extend my trembling hand. "Have you had some?"

"Of course I've had some. Go ahead. You have to."

The water was ice cold, delicious, and could not have tasted more pure—not that I was concerned about whether it actually was. I began feeling better as the first sip slipped down my throat. Magic potion. Kiss of a prince. Another sip and my surroundings came into focus. I walked to the edge of the bank and looked out. Was this Trout Brook? Alder Brook? Or a different stream altogether? We had no idea.

One thing you lose when you are lost, in life, in the forest, or wandering through a convoluted city in your car, is perspective, context, a sense of relationships: how this connects to that. You become unable, like the Mbuti in the rain forest, to see beyond the figurative nose in front of your face. If you could see the context, perceive relationships in "the right" perspective, you would not be lost. When you can perceive the whole, you can find your way, *a* way, back to the known. In the best circumstances, perspective reveals that what appears to be chaos is actually order. At worst, it becomes evident that what appears to be chaos is exactly as it seems.

A stream in the forest, as a constant among myriad variables, would, at the very least, we thought, provide us with a place we could see out of in the most literal sense of the Latin root *perspicere*: to regard, investigate, ascertain. It would be a window into the wider world that would provide us with a context. This didn't happen. What I did find reassuring was the stream's meandering: it suggested there was somewhere to go, that almost anything, familiar or unfamiliar, near or far from home, could reveal itself as we rounded the next bend.

And as we stood puzzling over how to decide which bend was the most promising, from somewhere across the water we heard the sound some call the Adirondack banjo. The sputter of a chain saw starting up is not altogether dissimilar to the choked awakening of a power lawn-mower, but a much more common sound here, where lawns are the exception and a need for woodcutting the rule. Seconds later, from more or less the same direction, we heard the rumble of a heavy vehicle on a paved road. Civilization! Upstream or down? We listened. One's sense of the locus of sound is rarely reliable in the echo chamber of a forest, but it seemed to be coming from downstream. Downstream we went.

We followed the dry bank for a short distance, carefully scanning the opposite shore. It remained inscrutable, wild. Soon the narrow path deteriorated into more alder swamp, and as we inched along, try-ing more or less blindly for the best footing, we were forced away from the stream. Still, the further we walked, the closer the sounds of the chain saw and the road became. At one point, they seemed almost near enough to touch. Yet there was no way to get to them, or even to see beyond the scratchy bush in which we were once more entrapped. Closer, further, closer, they stayed with us, the raspy saw and the droning trucks, invisible as the barred owl had been last night.

Close your eyes. Listen. Imagine where you are. What you see is some version of a green lawn on a still summer's day, some sort of modest house a few yards from where you stand. A garden, perhaps; flowers, vegetables. Maybe an apple tree beginning to set fruit. A driveway, a car, possibly a garage, a stack of firewood, a lawnmower, any of the genteel trappings of civilized life. Open your eyes. The sounds continue, but the place? What is this place? The suburbs? The tropics? There is nothing to be seen but an impenetrable wood.

The sodden air is absolutely still, the sky a cloudless blue. The alder swamp is thinning out. We approach its edge, anticipating more solid footing as it curves away from the stream. With each step, I expect the ground to meet my feet with a more reassuring firmness. Instead, the ground feels precarious and squishy. Wetness seeps inside my boots. We step beyond the last of the alders. Streamside, there is no dry bank, but an expanse of waist-high grass, a brilliant, sharp-edged grass of an extraordinary clear green against a blue, blue sky. In the distance, a faint, almost indiscernible ribbon of darker blue meets the horizon. The grass is growing in water.

Drenched in sweat, we stood in full sun, gaping at the long green grass. It felt as if hours had passed since we'd left the dark hemlocks of the streambank. Without catching even a glimpse of the dry land that supported the chain saw and the trucks (all out of earshot now) we'd struggled through all that alder only to reach open wetland.

"Well, now what?" I sighed.

Bob muttered something under his breath.

Knowing him as long as I do, I don't need to hear words, but only to catch a certain edge to his voice to understand he's not to be reasoned with. It was his turn to panic.

"What did you say?" I asked quietly, trying to sound as if we were sitting at some kitchen table, each lost in our respective reading. I didn't actually care what he'd said. I was stalling for time.

"I don't know 'what now,' but there's no way I'm walking through that shit again," he snarled.

"We can't cross this," I insisted.

"Well then what? What? Turn back and get scratched blind in that mess we just went through? We've got to get across."

I, too, was dismayed to think of retracing our steps, but if nothing was growing in this swamp but grass, it meant there was too much water to support anything bigger—including me.

"We can't cross this," I repeated calmly.

"Maybe we can. I'll check it out."

This was fine with me, but as soon as I lost sight of him in the marsh, I began to wonder if he'd come back. Just stay here, I told myself firmly. If he loses his way out there, he'll find you eventually if you just stay put.

When I saw him again, his jeans were soaked and muddy almost to the waist. Far as he'd gone, he hadn't been able to see the stream.

"Well you were right. We're fucked. Any suggestions?" he demanded, as if it were my fault. I ignored this.

"We turn around," I said. "Go back to where we drank the water, and head upstream. At least we're not wandering around in a bloody circle." That much seemed perfectly clear. I expected resistance but, gratefully, got none.

4

One of the things you think about when you are missing is who will miss you. However hopelessly lost you may be, you aren't, in fact, missing, until someone does. We weren't expected anywhere. No one knew our habits (did we really have any?) or had reason to keep track of our whereabouts. Those who knew us well would be quicker to assume we'd gone off hiking than met with foul play. But where would we have gone? There was no one who, missing us eventually, would guess we might have headed for the farm.

Even our nearest neighbor, Jim, who often knew what we were up to, wouldn't have a clue. Jim was retired and sufficiently disabled by heart disease that he had a self-imposed prohibition against venturing into the woods on foot. But he did a variety of odd jobs, from electrical work and carpentry to chauffeuring and cooking for an elderly lady in the next town and making a weekly round trip of nearly 200 miles to deliver a local baker's bread to an Albany restaurant. There were times when our paths crossed with Jim's several times a day, but he'd had a lot of work that summer. Though I'd been hearing his car rumble across the bridge each morning at about 7:45, neither Bob nor I had seen him in two weeks.

The presence of our car in the driveway, I mused, would narrow the possibilities only somewhat, since we could access a number of routes into the backcountry from our cabin on foot. Only the chicken I'd put out to defrost, rotting by now on the kitchen counter, would inevitably suggest to someone that we hadn't planned to be away for long.

Abruptly I stopped, and found myself embracing the trunk of the nearest tree for support. "Wait. Please," I called out. Confident as I'd been about the need to retrace our steps, I was disoriented. The sun's heat was pulsing through my head. We'd walked through another day. I felt sick with despair.

"We're going to have to stop soon," I said. "It's almost night."

"No, Bibi, no."

"Yes. We're going to have to spend another night out here, and if we do, I don't think we're going to make it."

"Oh, my word. No, Bibi, look. Look at the sky. It isn't anywhere close to night. Look where the sun is. It's still morning. It's about nine in the morning. Maybe not even that."

"That's impossible," I said. But I considered: at nine, we'd have been walking four or five hours without stopping for more than a moment or two. It wasn't unreasonable to feel tired. And of course, looking down, as I tended to do, I saw primarily the sameness of the forest light, while Bob the astronomer was looking at the sun.

It was time for a bit of trail mix. We'd been very conservative with that, and even now preferred taking only a nibble to finishing all we had left. But it's amazing what three peanuts, two raisins, six sunflower seeds and a quarter of a dried apricot can do to clear the brain. We walked on. And soon I remembered Dick. This was the morning our friend Dick was to come from Crown Point, nearly an hour away, to drop off scaffolding and finalize plans for replacing some windows in our cabin.

"Dick was supposed to come by today," I reminded Bob.

"What time?"

"Around ten, he said. Do you think he's there yet?"

"Probably not."

Adirondack time is a quirky variable. With some folks, it's elastic in the direction you might expect, with others, precise, while a few, unlike anyone I've met elsewhere, can be counted on to be early for appointments, sometimes by more than half an hour, with no explanation. Dick was one of the elastic ones. If he named an hour, which he rarely did, he might or might not be prompt. Usually, "in the morning," "after lunch," or "late afternoon" was as specific as he'd get. The meaning of breaking an appointment is different here than in

Manhattan, too, in the way that expectations about time and about what can be predicted and controlled in general are different in places where weather makes itself strongly felt. And just as it's rude to take up too much of people's time in Manhattan, one can't be in too much of a hurry here. The operative assumption is that time, like space, is abundant, and it's impolite to behave otherwise. So a bit goes to waste? No matter.

Bob, who has a gift for adapting seamlessly to new situations, quickly assimilated this style, and was already being taken for a native. I, however, still internalized an urban clock. If we'd been lost this morning in a car somewhere, I would have speculated about the remote possibility that we'd be able keep our appointment, about the consequences of our absence, how long Dick would wait, what he would think, would he be angry, how angry? until I worked my mind into a frenzied stew. In a car, I'd have felt as guilty about the possibility that I'd seriously inconvenienced Dick, who was seriously inconvenienced every day, as I would have been if I'd allowed myself to become delayed over something frivolous. But here, numbly putting one foot in front of the other, I had only one clear thought about Dick: he was not going to go looking for us or sound any alarms.

Dick, who'd lived in the Adirondacks most of his life, except for his Vietnam years, made a point of staying out of the woods except on his snowmobile or his bulldozer, and seemed honestly bewildered about our fascination with the forest. He'd be momentarily puzzled that we stood him up, maybe even concerned. But not sufficiently concerned to report our absence to anyone, for instance, his good friend Jerry, my brother, who was at this moment at his desk in the towering Manhattan offices of an international bank. However, if they happened to be talking....

The stream came into view beyond a dark veil of pines. We'd picked our way through the alders much more quickly this time, I thought. Reaching the bank, we looked up and down, exactly as we had before, as if the vista might have changed, as if new alternatives might have miraculously appeared. But of course nothing had changed, and since we'd already walked downstream, there was nothing to decide.

We followed a natural corridor along the bank, flanked by hemlock and pine, about three feet above the water. It was the kind of path one often finds among healthy conifers of some age. The lower branches are sparse, while the canopy is dense, shielding the forest floor from sun and thus discouraging most understory plants: there's room to move. Such streamside paths are often very pretty. This one was, and across the stream, what might have been its mirror image was full of grace and mystery. It was the kind of spot we might have sought out and enjoyed, but neither of us mumbled a syllable about how nice it was. My mind's erratic compass kept trying to link this place with a part of Jim's land we'd bushwhacked through last year. A bit of scuffling through the worst kind of brambly, burnt out clearcut had rewarded us with a little stand of white pine like this, and beyond, a wide, marshy section of Trout Brook. In a dim corner of my mind I was seeking confirmation of this hunch, waiting for this place to become that swampy spot, a paradise of insects and warblers which would have put us only ten minutes or so from home. In the foreground of my attention, however, were balsams and Scotch pines. Though there were none in sight, we were now moving in the direction of those I'd seen earlier, and remembering them gave me hope.

The sandy path, just wide enough to put one foot in front of the other, twined around a sharp bend. Though Bob was a few yards ahead of me, it seemed we both saw it at once: from the opposite shore, a narrow dock jutted into the stream. In the full sun, its pine boards were new-looking, almost white. Beyond the dock, the brush had been mowed back. We were looking at a pastoral scene that might have been the edge of someone's green lawn.

"I know where we are," Bob said casually, as if he'd just cruised through a brief moment of confusion. "I've been here in the canoe."

"Then it's Trout Brook?"

"It's Trout Brook."

We couldn't say how far our cabin was, or how difficult it would be to get there, but we were heading in the right direction.

It was only then that we realized that the small dock was the first sign of human presence, apart from the logging roads themselves, that we'd seen since dusk when we abandoned the last faded blaze and began our descent from the beech forest. Apart from those roads, the blazes and the cairns, it was the only human-made thing we'd seen since we'd left the farm. Even down below—that other "down below" last night, where nearly every inch of ground was marked by the passage of men and possibly women—we hadn't seen a beer can, a cigarette butt, a flip-top ring, a spent shell, a plastic collar from a six-pack, the vestiges of a campfire gone cold decades past.

We have seen such things, bits of them, virtually everywhere we've been. Their absence here seemed odd, suggesting we'd come through country even more remote than we had sensed it to be. Though this unintelligible tangle of public/private land embraced no major hiking trail or backcountry peak, we'd thought at least some of it was popular hunting ground. Further, it was the kind of Adirondack place where one sometimes finds the rusted remains of entire households hauled in long ago by folks requiring a larger range than most, determined to live, at least for a time, in isolation. I was never sure if such a vestigial household belonged to a lone hermit, or a couple, even a family. What rusted bits remained always suggested to me rather a lot of stuff for one person to bring in. And these things, including bedsprings, cookstoves, pots and pans, usually lay in places where it was impossible to fathom how anyone—even a great Paul Bunyan of a someone—had transported them. I'd wonder how long it might have taken the forest to so thoroughly erase even the suggestion of a road passable by motor vehicle or carriage—or if perhaps such households were hauled in by sled in early winter. To an archeologist they'd probably be an open book, but to me the twisted bedsprings, bits of doors and windows, the slate blue agateware utensils worn through with holes (rusting here for thirty years or one hundred?) tell a tale as sparse and enigmatic about the lives of those who brought them to the forest as Southwestern cliff dwellings tell about long-vanished races. They evoke the same questions, too: What drew or drove them here? How long did they remain? Were the forest hermits and the cliff-dwellers driven by the same thing or a different one—death itself?—to abandon their homes and move on, or back, to another world?

The opposite shore was wild and empty again. But what was that shimmering in the moss at my feet? Glass? An old wine bottle! Yes, I was happy, outrageously so, at the sight of garbage in the woods! The sign of my species.

Deadfall and underbrush were forcing us away from the water. But that was okay. As long as we kept the stream to our left, we'd be fine. The knowledge that it was there—a true anchor point—lightened my step as we bushwhacked through a thick, dusty wood. Bob was ahead of me, just beyond my view, when he called out, "I'm on a road! An old woods road!"

I scrambled through the brush until I could see a bit of his blue plaid shirt. "Wait for me," I called, almost breathless. "Wait!"

It was a road all right, not rutted and raw like the logging roads below, but smooth and dry as our driveway. Here and there, a balsam spired through the surrounding hardwoods, here and there, a few Scotch pines. The road eventually faded to a path, lumpy and pitted, uphill and down, crossed now and again by rivulets, blowdowns, brambles, dotted in dry places with white tufts of pearly everlasting in the first days of its long bloom. The walking was rough, far rougher than in the trackless beech grove, but it was a clear path nonetheless.

After a time, it led through a berry patch—red raspberries, ripe, abun-
dant—as many red raspberries as I'd ever seen growing in one place.
Though we must have needed food, we didn't pause to graze but just
snatched a few berries in passing. We were moving fast now, and
hunger was not what was driving us. The possibility of getting out was
so near we couldn't stop. If this is another dead end, I thought, we'll
come back here and eat berries.

The long, deep berry patch faded to scrubland: blueberry, barren
or past fruiting, steeplebush, meadowsweet, early goldenrod. Then, at
a high spot, the path opened into a road again and spread through a
sandy clearing that had long settled into its ways. Once the trees had
been cut for farming, the farming failed and abandoned, neither trees
nor much of anything else had grown again.

Just before this clearing met its pine-shaded edge, we rounded
a bend and saw that not far ahead, the woods road ended. From
twenty yards away, below the wall of trees that marked the end of our
path, we saw only a patch of brown earth we wouldn't have noticed if
the sun hadn't been spotlighting a little bare area, its irregular shape
outlined by a scraggly edge of knee-high grass, sparse, barely a tickle
at the shins. It wasn't until we were right there, about to step into what
appeared to be a streak of sunlight on the forest floor, that its lineari-
ty and then its extent revealed itself: another dirt road.

It was a little wider than the one on which we'd intersected it, at
this point possibly driveable, and in something lighter than a logging
truck. Was this what we thought it might be? No. We paused, looked
right, then left. We saw nothing noteworthy, nothing familiar at all. It
looked no more like a road people live on than any path or old
carriage road in the deep woods.

We permitted ourselves only one certainty: we were walking
downhill on a dirt road cut through mixed forest. The road curved
and curved again, unfolding slowly. At no point could we see more
than a few yards ahead.

It was not even when we saw the first power pole, but only when we were up next to that pole, where an official metal street sign says "Williams Drive" in whimsical reference to the short driveway of a little hunting camp owned by a man named Williams, that doubt flew off. We glanced up the drive at the tidy white cabin, the rusted Jeep out front, the rounded fender of the vintage Chevy pickup, half-buried and surely at its eternal rest, among the wild rose.

All this we had seen hundreds of times before. In minutes, we'd be home.

I was stunned that we hadn't known it sooner, the moment we saw the end of the woods road—no, before. That sandy clearing we'd come to after the berry patch: hadn't we been there, too? If it was the place I now suspected, we'd wandered there at least half a dozen times, in spring, in summer, under a foot of snow. Yet, the possibility that we were on familiar ground hadn't even occurred to me as we were passing through.

Now surely, if you were dropped blindfolded from a helicopter a quarter mile from your home, you would know where you were when you removed the blindfold. Wouldn't you? I am still perplexed that, on that August morning, yearning so for something that we knew, we didn't recognize our road—and weren't even sure it was a real road.

Have you ever looked into a familiar face and seen a stranger? *I don't know you. Do I?* A dead parent encountered in a dream, an old friend very much alive—is looking at you directly, eyes quizzical, "Don't you know me?" The voice is amazed, amused, slightly teasing. But the person into whose face you're dumbly peering isn't sure whether to laugh or cry or shake you by the shoulders.

One morning in the city I'd walked downtown on some errand, then picked up the subway two stops south of my usual station. On my way to deliver a magazine assignment and lunch with an editor, I was profoundly preoccupied. When I emerge from months of work on a complicated piece of writing, I typically feel as if I'm crawling out of a cave. But today there was more on my mind. Bob's father, hospitalized with a broken bone, had just contracted pneumonia and been transferred to intensive care, where we were to visit him that afternoon. In still another layer of thought, while descending from the street to the subway platform, I'd recalled a compelling dream from the previous night. I kept rolling it by so I could hang on to the details until the train arrived and I could sit and write it down. I thought about relating it to my therapist next Tuesday, and briefly considered whether it was possible to schedule an earlier session.

I boarded the train, sat down, started writing. A woman about my age in a frumpy down coat took the seat next to me. I edged over, kept writing. Felt her looking at me. Slightly annoyed, I looked up into her face.

"Bibi," she said to me, incredulous, "don't you know me?"

I didn't. I looked and looked. Noted the contour of her cheekbone, her hazel eyes. I still didn't.

"You really don't know me."

I shook my head, tried to smile.

"Janet," she finally said.

Janet. Janet? Janet?!!!

She was my therapist. I'd last seen her three days ago. She'd boarded the train at this station because she lived and worked about a hundred yards away.

Whatever this marks in my psychological state, I believe I failed to recognize Janet, who'd been in my thoughts seconds before she appeared, because I was accustomed to seeing her in one context only. Though she was practically a neighbor, our paths never crossed. I had never seen her outside her office, never seen her in a coat. And as I am accustomed to recognizing places by their landmarks, so I am in the habit of identifying people by their clothes. If asked what kind of coat Janet would be wearing on the way to shop for dollhouse furniture at

Macy's at 11:30 on a Friday morning in mid-December, I'd never have put her in that dowdy mauve down thing, but in a stylish cloth coat, black.

To encounter familiar ground out of context is far more rare than meeting a familiar person in an unexpected place. We are never required to identify the street we live on from a lineup. Still, it would never have occurred to me that I could fail to do so. After so many leaps to reshape the strange to the familiar, seeking pattern where there was none, inventing relationships where we couldn't perceive them, trying to discern or at worst imagine our surroundings when it was indeed impossible to see the forest for the trees, Bob and I were both reluctant to name this place as the way out of the woods.

We'd reversed ourselves, turned the familiar into the strange. And this seemed a marvelous thing.

As marvelous as the fact that we were no longer lost.

Lost. Not a dream, but it felt like one. Yet the return felt even more unreal.

The first thing I saw when we opened the door was a flat package lying in the middle of the living room floor where it must have landed when the FedEx driver opened the screen door and tossed it into the house. I knew what was in the package: material sent by my editor for a magazine piece I was allegedly working on. My so-called real life. This life seemed to belong to someone else, about whom I knew nothing and in whom I had not the slightest interest.

Had we actually perished in the woods? Was it only our ghosts who opened the old screen door to our cabin that morning?

The man and woman who entered the house sat down at the dining table within moments with cups of strong hot coffee, lit cigarettes.

"I feel like we should call someone to tell them we're all right," Bob said.

I shook my head. "There's no one to call. No one knows we were gone."

Having eschewed an answering machine, my umbilicus for ten months of the year, we didn't know if anyone had phoned us.

The clock on the mantle told us it was a few minutes before ten. Dick was not there and there was no sign he had been. Things, exactly as we'd left them, were a mess. The dining table that became a catch-all because it was the only real table in the cabin was strewn with the usual unrelated accouterments of our lives in progress—a hammer, a week-old *New York Times,* a box of wooden matches, an empty potato chip bag, the things you might find there at any time.

On the kitchen counter, the chicken I'd left to defrost lay benign-looking enough, invisibly en route to an advanced state of decay, who knows what bacteria multiplying with each passing moment.

The comfort of our modest shelter, a rough-hewn cabin built with logs cut from the land on which its cinderblock foundation rests, had the obscene opulence of an excessively rich dessert.

Breakfast at the diner, always a celebratory treat, seemed in order. Bob wrote a note for Dick telling him to join us there, and tacked it to the outside door, which he then closed. Five minutes later, I was sitting "in town" at the diner's sunny window, sipping my second cup of coffee, waiting for bacon and eggs while Bob ran across the street to the general store for the newspaper. It seemed so ridiculously easy, life. Also absurd that we could spend sixteen hours or so as we had, and then come back and merely resume. I wondered if all those disembodied feelings were a product of lack of food. An insufficient flow of glucose to the brain? But after devouring breakfast, I didn't feel any more grounded inside the body that was relishing all these routine activities.

There was something eerily familiar about this disjunction. For as long as I can remember, I've occasionally imagined what it would be like to return after death, incorporeal, invisible, though I never pursue the fantasy very far before it becomes unbearably sad.

We drove home. Eventually Dick came. I took business calls and calls from family and colleagues who had no idea we'd been inaccessible for a time, and finally, about 1 p.m. a call from my daughter, who phoned frequently that summer from Salt Lake City. She had called the night before, and was now relieved to find us home. If no one else knew, *she* knew that we were rarely away from the cabin at night. "If you hadn't been there today, I would have done something," she told me. I was confident that even from 2,000 miles away, she'd have done the best anyone could do to make sure we were found. And though we were home and safe, I was profoundly comforted to know that someone would have begun looking for us soon.

I'd been gazing out a window as we talked, half aware of the graying sky, but I was startled when the rain came, with crashing thunder and in a torrent. The telephone line began to crackle. I quickly hung up.

Bob had fallen asleep on the couch where he'd been reading the newspaper. I covered him with a blanket, closed the windows, stood at the screen door for a few minutes watching the rain drive thousands of tiny puddles into the sandy lawn, then headed for bed. As soon as I began unlacing my shoes, I found myself luxuriating in the multiplicity of sensations that accompany this ordinary act which I'd performed so many thousands of times, if only rarely in midafternoon in the dark of a thunderstorm: getting into bed! Releasing my body from the constraints of clothing, covering myself in some soft, loose garment, stretching out all the muscles in my limbs and back. A pillow under my head, all the blankets I needed to be warm, I closed my eyes and let my weariness sink into the mattress. Instantly the bed began to soak it from me, absorbing every ache and twinge to leave me lightly afloat on a raft of rest, its perfection sealed by the symphony of thunder and lightning outside.

Again, I was flooded with images of opulence. What extravagant splendor this was! Like winning a luxury car, something I never think of, or—more in tune with my usual material fantasies—slipping into the weightless sumptuousness of a fine cashmere coat. Getting into bed to go to sleep. My last thought as I drifted off was how lucky I was —not merely to have such cozy shelter from the rain when I so easily might have been out there—but because I had been jarred, however briefly, from inattention and had been given the opportunity to savor the fullness of the everyday, and to descend toward dream from a deep knowledge of safety and contentment. Home.

PART III

Home

*The space we love is unwilling to
remain permanently enclosed. It deploys
and appears to move elsewhere without
difficulty, into other times and on
different planes of dream and memory.*

The Poetics of Space, Gaston Bachelard

*Aboriginal creation myth tells of
legendary totemic beings who had
wandered over the continent in
the Dreamtime, singing out the name
of everything that crossed their path—
birds, animals, plants, rocks,
waterholes—and so singing the
world into existence.*

Songlines, Bruce Chatwin

5

There are places where people go to disappear.

The Adirondack Park is such a place on a grand scale: a forested mountainous dome nearly as large as the state of Massachusetts. On early English maps of New York, it was a blank spot. The Dutch believed the area was inhabited by unicorns. The Iroquois and Algonquin who occasionally hunted there called it *Couxsachrage*, which means "dismal wilderness" or "habitation of winter." For Europeans, it remained *terra incognita*, virtually unexplored until the nineteenth century. Even today, its wild rivers, secluded valleys and secret lakes, embraced by formidable mountains and dense boreal forests, remain defiant of roadbuilding and agriculture, steeped in mystery.

When Bob and I began looking for a house, we imagined a place where we could be found only when we wanted to be, where there were no other people, where, though we never articulated it, we could play Adam and Eve in the garden. And, much like the painters and writers who were beguiled by the Adirondacks in the nineteenth century, we'd idealized the rugged mountain forest as a pristine wilderness with no significant human presence. In all our hiking and camping trips, we'd encountered nothing to dispel this fantasy.

We spent our first night in the Adirondacks in a tent in a state campground. In the next tent were my brother Jerry, and his seven-year-old son David. With the rest of the family—my daughter Elizabeth, Jerry's wife Rosemary and their older son Toby—we graduated from state campgrounds to backcountry sites, then returned to the campgrounds for long weekends that combined hiking with househunting. We began by looking for a place that could accommodate all seven us, but all the places we were shown required renovations far beyond our means or desires. Smaller houses in reasonable condition were much more plentiful. Jerry and Rosemary settled on a modest, fifteen-year-old house built on the secluded site of an old farm in a town called Paradox. Bob and I kept looking.

Most city dwellers who want a country place want it no more than a couple of hours from town. That we were seeking a getaway some 250 miles from our apartment struck many of our friends as odd. But it made sense for us. Bob wanted dark nights, a sky on which he could train his telescope unimpeded either by local street lamps or a glow on the horizon from some populous community. As for me, having lived for ten years about a hundred miles from New York City in the Hamptons with its moneyed sheen and high-pitched social buzz, I didn't want another rural extension of Manhattan. I wanted a place in which I could shuck city life like an old skin.

We couldn't make the five hundred mile round trip every week-end, but for a freelancer and a teacher with two months off in the summer and lots of holidays throughout the year, that seemed fine. The many weekends in town would permit us to maintain some sort of city life, and from time to time, to briefly disappear.

On a gloomy Saturday in March, stung by a light freezing rain that had little impact on the heavy snow cover, Bob and I took our first walk on the land we now think of as ours. By then, we'd been looking at Adirondack property for years. We'd rejected grim mobile homes and pleasant cottages at busy intersections and old farmhouses that promised to consume every spare dime for the rest of our lives.

We'd never been shown anything like this.

From the edge of the lawn that fronted a tiny log cabin built by a local man and his friends in the 1950s, we looked down a small slope to an effusive stream. The water was nearly as wide as our Manhattan street, and on the other side stood a wall of stately trees—white pine, balsam fir, hemlock, cedar, red spruce—verdant and lush even in this latitude's drabbest season, and all but mute about any human habitat they might conceal.

The one visible mark of the civilized world was a weathered picnic table nestled on a little rise a few yards from the shore. That picnic table worried us. On our second visit, when the snow was gone, we descended the narrow stone and cedar staircase that led from the lawn to the water, and from the grassy "beach" scarcely big enough for two sunbathers, we studied that lonely gray table across the stream as if it could foretell the future. Imagine that table laden with food and beer on a hot, bright day, pressed about by half a dozen people, talking and laughing, scampering in and out of the water....

The property across the stream, the real estate agent told us, belonged to a couple with three teenage daughters, and that the family used the place only once or twice a year. Their house was well-maintained, even smaller than the one we thought to buy, built over a trailer with siding stained a subdued dark red. It couldn't be seen from this side of the stream, even when we were standing at the water's edge. No, the agent didn't know where they lived year-round. Maybe Pennsylvania?

But by then, it was a moot point. Bob had fallen in love with the cabin. There was an instant appeal in the warmth of the simple, hand-hewn structure and the beauty of its setting: balsam spires silhouetted on the sky, the deep greens of winter trees against the snow, the way the forest framed a little clearing for cabin and stream view. All of this conspired to obscure from our consideration the expense of the immediate need for a new roof and foundation. Most important, the place was well-hidden from the dirt road, at the end of a driveway so obscure we'd failed to find it the first time we came looking. It appeared to promise the isolation we sought. Clearly, these six acres guaranteed privacy less surely than a larger piece of land. But none of the bigger properties we'd seen had so moved us to believe it could be our Eden. Given that there were vast wildlands nearby, we decided to take our chances for brook music and the smell of balsam. Still, either you're in love or you're not, and I wasn't.

Early on, we'd dutifully committed to paper the property's attributes and failings. Nineteen fell on the plus side, compared to thirteen on the minus—a silly, mechanical equation I found somewhat reassuring. But my problem wasn't so much about the cabin's obvious drawbacks—tiny windowless kitchen, no closets, and less square footage than our city apartment, to name a choice few. The problem was, I loved another place and, through our first summer here and into the second, remained secretly heartbroken to have forsaken it.

The place I loved was less than twenty miles away. It was not a specific house or plot of land, but a great wild space crisscrossed by a few narrow, breathtakingly lonely roads, settled, farmed and mined after the Civil War, abandoned by the turn of the century, and now, at the turn of the next, inhabited only by a huge variety of birds, wildflowers and furred mammals, and a scant handful of reclusive humans. It was a remote corner of the township of Paradox—so-named for a stream that, under certain conditions, reverses direction and flows back toward its source.

For nearly five years, Jerry and Rosemary's vacation house in Paradox had been our Adirondack base, bringing us to the mountains in winter for the first time. Here, Bob and I had landscaped and planted and weeded—neither Jerry nor Rosemary had had the opportunity to stick their hands in soil before—and the four of us produced prodigious gardens in the old cow pasture. And we had all manner of good times together, wandering the valley by day or night, in every light, at every season. Infinitely generous, Jerry and Rosemary might have put up with us as part of the household indefinitely. Still, we needed our own place.

The day after we took possession of the cabin, as we drove out of Paradox with a few boxes we'd stored at my brother's house, I felt a weight of sorrow I couldn't then put into words. All through the half-hour drive to our new place, on roads we'd traveled hundreds of times, the heaviness in my heart said I would never, could never, return, when in fact I could return the next day, or any time I chose to. It was not the house, nor the extended family that I mourned leaving. It was the land: those infinite woods we could never know if we roamed them every day of our lives.

But it was not as if I had two suitors to choose between. Rather, my first love hadn't quite offered his hand—though the chance he might one day do so remained a disturbing tease.

Few houses of any description ever came on the market in Paradox, so we'd looked at acreage. Several big, remote pieces proved to be teeming with hunters in and out of season. A more manageable one was withdrawn from sale; another was firmly priced at twice its value. Jerry and Rosemary would have sold us fifteen acres, but we would have had to cut a half mile of driveway through the forest to reach it. This made me uncomfortable from the beginning, and ultimately, felt wrong to all of us as we considered the impact of such cutting on the surrounding woods and its creatures.

The more we thought about it, the less inclined we were to chop up any forest to put up a house; it made more ecological sense to purchase land with an existing structure, even a shell. But if we wanted to buy in Paradox, we'd have to wait. And wait. Bob was impatient. His parents had died within two years of each other, and he and his sister had sold the family home to which he'd been deeply attached. He needed new roots. And I, with a short story collection near completion, was more than ready to escape our noisy apartment and take a whole summer just to write.

The day we decided to look beyond Paradox, we were directed to the cabin.

There was a crucial period when negotiations were going badly, and it seemed we couldn't proceed. I had so many doubts, I was almost relieved. One Saturday morning, as we sat at our kitchen table in the city glumly speculating about the real estate lawyer's ominous silence, I said matter-of-factly, "Look, we may not be able to buy this place." Bob replied, "Right. But if we can't, I'll cry." I knew the time had come for me to at least temporarily hold my peace.

Within our first week at the cabin, two things told me that we were in a place very different from Paradox. One: the man who'd built our cabin, followed by two of its subsequent owners, then several current neighbors, appeared at our door "just to see who bought the place." No one we knew made impromptu social calls in Paradox. And, two, it was much harder to figure out where to take the mice.

White-footed mice, with their long nursery-rhyme tails and huge brown eyes, find their way into every Adirondack dwelling, and ours were undeterred by the two cats we'd brought along. Jerry and Rosemary had been evicting their mice with the aid of a harmless trap called the tin cat. They set the trap only when they were at home to release its captives, then simply drove them around the corner, which was two miles away, before letting them out in the woods, too far from any human's house for them to move indoors.

Our house essentially belonged to mice when we took over. We caught five the very first night, then realized there was no obvious place to let them go. There was plenty of wild land we could walk to, but we didn't care to walk far with metal boxes full of mice. And, though our new town had a distinctly remote character, there were houses, if mostly set far apart on large properties, everywhere within a ten minute drive. We understood, and not happily, that we hadn't exactly moved to the woods, but to a human neighborhood. What we didn't understand was that the two are not necessarily mutually exclusive.

By the end of the first summer, I was sure we'd made a mistake. Across the stream, the picnic table that had worried us remained unused and nearly invisible behind the season's foliage. But we were unprepared for the popularity of the bridge as a fishing spot. Sizeable fish were merely a memory here, but such a persistent one that the road virtually bustled at times. Suburbia, I'd called it in frustration. When people talked loudly on the bridge we could hear them inside the cabin with the windows closed. This occurred rarely; nonetheless, the message was clear: The privacy we usually enjoyed was fragile, and not within our control. And our place, albeit a perfect setting for the cozy forest tales of childhood, soon felt manicured—Bob's favorite landscape pejorative—tame, even hemmed in. I didn't think we'd stay.

Yes, there had been some transcendent moments: Sitting by the brook, watching the light on the water. Splashing in the swimming hole and the fresh smell that clung to my hair afterwards. The way the cabin sat so neatly in the snow. The easy ways of folks in town. The quiet summer mornings when I lost myself in writing with the early sun streaming over me. But overall, I'd spent more time and emotion missing my first love than being happy to be here. I kept scanning the real estate ads for a property I liked better, not really knowing what I was looking for, much less what I'd do if I found it.

Then we got lost in the woods. When we returned the next morning, something had changed.

For weeks afterwards, as I sat in my front yard, with Trout Brook burbling beyond the patchy grass, I kept turning and returning to the comfort of the hemlock against which I'd rested in the forest after gathering firewood, then to our little makeshift hearth, so simple, yet, in its way, complete. And I thought about the road, just out of view, that had led us to the farmhouse and beyond.

If this were a fairy tale, I thought, its conclusion would echo Little Red Riding Hood's chastened promise: "As long as I live, I will never again leave the path to run into the wood, when my mother has forbidden me to do so." Don't stray, don't stray. Go directly to Grandma's house. Come right home from school! As a child, I obeyed. As an adult, I seek exactly what I'm told to avoid. Out of the woods, in mind I found myself moving ever deeper into the forest.

Nearly six months passed before we actually went back up the road again. There was snow on the ground, the ideal light cover that makes for easier backcountry walking than summer's bare skin where logging's wooden bones protrude. Were these the same raspberry bushes that had borne such abundant, rosy fruit on that August morning? Or were the stark canes rising from the snow just another bramble patch, a stand of the tenacious blackberries that take hold in any bare place that affords a little sun? We had different opinions, too, about which of several old woods roads was the one that had led us out. Did we emerge across the road from that huge boulder? Impossible. Surely we'd have noticed this elephantine granite relic from the glacial age. Wouldn't we?

Like a couple doing a post-mortem on a fight, we couldn't reconcile our separate recollections to say, finally, *what really happened.* And our perceptions of which places in reality corresponded to those in memory didn't quite match up. But one thing we agreed on: Though we had at times been almost within shouting distance of the world beyond the woods, parts of that forest were as true a wilderness as any place we'd wandered in fifteen years together: the eminent domain of other creatures.

One day, Bob admitted, out of the blue. "I panicked that night in the beech forest. I read the compass wrong."

Yes.

But by then several of our neighbors had reported similar experiences: a hunter who'd stalked deer on the ridge since childhood, one of the owners of the old farm, others who'd lived their lives near these woods. Each of these folks had just wandered beyond the farm one day, got turned around somehow, and having planned to be out for an hour or so meandered uphill and down for five, eight or ten hours before finding Alder Brook as we had hoped to, crossing to the road and walking or hitching the ten odd miles home. They, too, were still shaking their heads over how this could have happened to them.

Several times, we retraced our steps up to a point, and tried in vain to watch the tape rewind.

I could place myself at the farm that evening, and up in the beech grove, but even after poring over maps and talking with old-timers in the neighborhood, I wasn't sure where we'd been that night in the bottomlands. I knew I could never find the hummock where we'd slept. I couldn't picture its relation to any other landmark or sense the direction we came from to find it or took to leave it. Surely it was out there somewhere still, the nest of hemlock boughs, the shredded mylar on the forest floor, the char of our small fire.

My focus shifted from the beech grove, and our mysterious little campsite to the fact that when we'd finally emerged from the woods less than half a mile from our driveway, we hadn't recognized our road. As even topographic maps reveal almost nothing of the forest's character and intensity, no map told that if left alone, the vegetable kingdom and all the animal life it shelters and sustains would not only embrace the road but reclaim it.

I thought I knew this place—the road and what lay on either side along the scant mile between our house and the farm. Now, I was caught up in its mysteries. Despite the countless times I'd walked there I hadn't been able to pick out a familiar rock or tree or flower at that crucial junction between being lost and understanding where we were. More intriguing, we hadn't recognized it as a *real* road, a mapped place distinct from the immensity of the forest through which we'd been traveling. Until we saw the first power pole, we hadn't known that we were out of the woods.

At the end of the looping, illogical track we'd made over sixteen hours or so in the forest, we truly had come to a new place. When the veil of familiarity lifted, our little house on our little swatch of land was no longer "not Paradox" but simply itself.

I became preoccupied with what it would mean to know this land: to have a name for every plant at every season, a mental map of each logging road and herd path, complete with cellar holes and old stone walls. And the birds, and all the mammals—the woodchucks and porcupines and rabbits and raccoons and deer and bear, the martens and fishers and minks and weasels, the foxes and coyotes—where did they spend the night?

How many layers in the birch bark?

Was it possible to know individually every tree larger than myself? What is that strange plant lushly leafing now in my new flower bed, unbidden? There are so many questions, some with answers, some without. The ubiquitous wild blackberries, for example, might be blackberries or dewberries. Probably they're both. As well as some (how many?) of the other variants of genus Rubus among the hundreds my field guide notes. Is that why, as they begin to ripen in late August, each bush looks different? Some at the penultimate stage have red berries, red canes, red leaves, some brown. When the berries ripen black, some are plump and pendulous with juice, while on other bushes, equally healthy in appearance, the fruit forms dry as buttons. What might science tell me about this? What is the folk wisdom? Is each and every berry different?

Some, surely, can name the moment of falling in love. Not I. But it was when the familiar became strange that my love for this place became possible. And as a yearning to know the other is one of the seeds of love, what eludes knowing is its nourishment.

With the sense that vast possibility lay at the edge of the lawn, my idea of home reorganized itself. I no longer perceived the locus of our cabin as just a suburb of a mountain village, or the bridge beyond as merely picturesque. When I understood, as I had not at the start, that the bridge carried the road away from civilization, it became a threshold from which I could explore the world. I stopped reading the real estate ads, and began to think about adding sticks to my nest.

6

"The neighborhood is changing." Spoken sotto voce, with a half-raised eyebrow I interpreted as something akin to a lewd wink, these words burned in my ears. I began hearing them when I was eight or so. I heard them no more after my family moved, when I was thirteen, from a shady side street in West Philadelphia to a new suburb, where change took the form of ever-increasing amenities.

In the confidential hiss of those words, I heard fear and anxiety I couldn't comprehend. But I knew their meaning: black people were buying the little row houses in our neighborhood, offered for sale mostly by growing families who had prospered heartily in the postwar boom, and were ready in the mid-fifties for suburban opulence. Our family hadn't prospered so much, but we went anyway. I didn't understand why anyone objected to black people moving in, or what there was to fear, and my sensibility rebelled at the sound of euphemistic vagueness, exactly as it did when adults used the same sort of terms, with similarly raised eyebrows, when bodily parts and functions were discussed.

I was a grown woman, indeed, my daughter was a grown woman, before I experienced what it meant to care about change in a neighborhood. Sometimes reckless in forming quick and firm attachments to people, I had always stood somewhat aloof from place. Even while owning a home and staying put there for a decade, and later living even longer in one rented apartment, I'd cultivated detachment.

Stories of the lost places of my father's war-torn Europe, interwoven with the bathetic losses of grand opera, filled my ears from birth; I wasn't taught much about what lasts, what you can keep. My refugee father set foot on American soil days before war was declared in Europe, and has remained amazed and grateful for this throughout his life. My American-born mother had her own losses, and the opera lyrics my parents loved and taught me from such cheery works as *La Boheme* and *La Traviata*—"You and I will find a haven, you and I together"—of a nested future almost achieved, thwarted by death or fate, were literally my nursery rhymes. No sooner is the haven in view, than it is forever lost.

So I easily grew into a habit of regarding every home as temporary, a habit perpetuated first by the sense of loss that permeated my favorite teenage reading—Poe, the Brontes, Thomas Wolfe—and later, by the writer's fantasy of life-changing news in tomorrow's metaphorical mail. This permitted me to be comfortable with the uncomfortable, to ignore the ugly and accept the unacceptable, to make some sort of nest anywhere, without investing much self or feeling and certainly no love—except in places that, like Paradox, I could not call mine.

Over time, I'd come to understand that, as difficult as it had been for me to settle on buying the cabin, it had been easier for me to move into a house I didn't love than into one I did. Since I'd operated on the premise that, if you're going to move forward in life, you must be willing to lose your place, some part of me had needed home to be a place I could walk away from as painlessly as I'd left the mylar-lined nest we'd made the night we were lost in the woods.

So it made no sense that I balked at referring to our cabin the way others, including Bob, did, as a camp. To me, the term diminished our place, though in the Adirondacks it carries no such intent. Historically, a camp could be anything from a hermit's hut to a sprawling compound of buildings grand in scale if rustic in style. In the Adirondacks, rustic is seldom synonymous with crude. What it describes is a building or artifact that makes a seamless transition with the forest. This is typically accomplished with exterior finishes of woodsy browns, accented by dark greens or reds, and by bringing the outdoors inside, with fieldstone fireplaces and wood furnishings that, incorporating bark or twigs or natural shapes, evoke the trees from which they were hewn. Historically, "camp life" was about roaming the woods unhampered by possessions and worries other than those of the moment. What could have suited me more?

Actually, what I resisted about "camp" is exactly what I should have liked best: it denotes temporary shelter. Whether spacious and commodious, or lacking the simplest amenities, a camp is a place you break down or close down and leave, to return or not in another season. But I couldn't bear to think of the cabin as something less than my true and only home.

I'm often asked when we close down our house for the season. In fact, we don't. The plumbing is set up so that it takes us five minutes to drain the pipes and pour anti-freeze down the traps each time we leave in the winter, and perhaps ten to turn the system on again when we return a few weeks later. Throughout the year, we come and go—a long weekend now and then, a week in Christmas, a week in February, and two months in the summer. When it's just a weekend, the four to six hour trip each way is both tiresome and tiring. But no visit seems too brief to be worth the effort. Sometimes it seems we do nothing all weekend but look around, yet that in itself feels as necessary as breathing. Sometimes I don't realize how much I need it until I'm here, soaking up the quiet like a desiccated sponge. Sometimes I feel like I'm reuniting with a lover after a separation filled with longing. In the first moments, actually seeing and touching the object of my yearning has an edge of unreality. And I am constantly alert for the most minute changes.

In my Manhattan neighborhood, change is a constant to which I pay little attention. Shops and restaurants come and go, and new languages routinely join the cacophony of the streets. Returning at summer's end, I check to see which stores have closed and what's replaced them: usually there's a new bank or another chain drug store, instead of independent shops where I actually bought stuff—the Caribbean deli that made better espresso than Starbucks for a fraction of the price, the shoe repair place, the most convenient greengrocer. In the vicinity of the cabin, however, anything that hints at change throws me into a fluster. I worry and wonder if a wildflower I'd picked last summer fails to reappear in the same spot. I keep a sharp ear for any activity on the bridge. Especially in the first few years, I'd fret about what it meant that there were people somewhere up the hill. Were they planning to stay? When our neighbor, Jim, declared a two-hour war on red squirrels and I realized that crossing the bridge would put me in his shotgun's path, I felt like a prisoner behind a guarded gate. Ultimately, however, all such disruptions proved temporary, inconsequential. Until suddenly, less than three years after our adventure beyond the farm, the character of the road was transformed: not, as I had fuzzily imagined it, absorbed into the forest, but ripped open by logging and surveyed into lots.

Despite my weak sense of permanence, all my life, I'd regarded trees as a feature of landscape that, barring encounter with nature's more violent extremes, would last "forever"—perhaps not with the longevity of mountains, but here before we came and to remain long after: venerable ancestors, whose lives would continue for generations beyond our own. Indeed, the earth's oldest trees, the bristlecone pines of California, have a lifespan of more than 4,000 years, long enough to witness the rising and setting of a million suns.

Today, I sit on my lawn and just beyond the rushing stream, with its Heraclitean paradox of change and sameness, peace and urgency, I hear trees falling.

I hear their spines crack and in those splintering trunks I imagine I can hear the cracking of my bones. I am, as it happens, recovering from a broken bone. I did not hear it break last week when, out for a moment to buy potatoes for dinner, I tripped over my churning thoughts and fell while crossing my Manhattan street, twisting my leg so radically it caused a hairline fracture in my hip.

It's a horrible sound to me, this cracking and splintering. Not a brutal snap like the gunfire I've heard in the city, but slower, an aching rasp sustained by an underlying moan.

I remind myself that in another age, to those who cleared land for farm and homestead, perhaps even on this sunny spot where soft grass brushes my feet, the falling tree sounded a note of triumph. So naive, my idea of the "eternal forest." Yet, like many naive beliefs, it has been held at one time or another everywhere in the world. The ancient Greeks believed the souls of the dead lived in trees, and that it was from trees that the human race was created. Trees everywhere have been regarded as the homes of all kinds of spirits. Perhaps it makes a certain simple, anthropocentric, pre-Copernican sense to think that because the natural lifespan of most trees is longer than ours, they will "always" be there.

Unfair, I think, that trees should be so vulnerable to our whims, needs, desires. But nature is no democracy. Fairness is fragile in any hierarchy, and nature's is no exception. The animal kingdom has dominion over the plant kingdom—at least most of the time, in most places.

The Martin family, who owned the old farm at the top of the hill visited it so rarely, it was only toward the end of our second summer here, some weeks after our night in the woods, that we first met some of them.

Early one morning I was walking on the road as I often did, following the seductive voices of birds with my binoculars. I must have ventured a little way into the woods because I didn't hear the truck that appeared suddenly, parked in the middle of the road. As I came down the hill and rounded a bend, there it was, shiny and black, with two men standing behind it. I'd never seen them before, but I knew at once who they were. Jim, who kept track of all the comings and goings along the road, had mentioned that the Martins would be around. They always phoned him before they came, he'd told us, in part just to assure him that they were the source of any activity he might be aware of on the hill, and also to find out about road conditions and how far up they could drive before the ruts and gullies became too daunting. Jim had alerted us to their presence several times before, but we'd always missed them. Now here they finally were in the flesh, two lean, striking men, more than six and a half feet tall. Ernie, a land surveyor in his late seventies, was a little bowed but powerful looking, with thick steely hair—an older version of Jason Robards Jr. but more massive. His son Herman, about thirty-five I guessed, was straight and slender, with close-cropped brown hair and warm brown eyes. He was reorganizing some cargo, while his father buttoned up a crisp, white shirt.

Now, any white shirt is anomalous in the Adirondacks, but this was a shirt white enough to outdazzle any at a black-tie ball. And the man in it had an elegant bearing unremarkable in the ballroom perhaps, but something you'd notice on a dusty road at the edge of nowhere. Despite this, I detected a hint of embarrassment—as if buttoning a shirt over an undershirt was too intimate an act in which to be surprised by a strange woman. In fact, both men's friendly faces registered a surprise I sensed was less a reaction to encountering another person where they thought they were alone, than to seeing a woman on this road where electricity was a recent luxury, and where, I later learned, none of the Martin women had set foot in years.

We introduced ourselves, chatted about the freshness of the morning and the special pleasures of being out and about so early in the day. Herman explained they'd been working in the woods since dawn, and that the mosquitoes were so fierce up at the farm, they'd decided to come down the hill a way to change clothes. I learned that Ernie had been widowed about two years, that Herman, older than I'd thought, was a newly retired military officer, now a graduate student, who had settled with his wife near Syracuse. They soon excused themselves: they had an appointment at the county seat. I invited them to stop by later to meet Bob, but we missed them when they did, and it wasn't until the following summer that we saw them again.

First, Herman came, unannounced, to pay a social call. I was in the house. I heard a vehicle, looked out the window, thought I'd seen the shiny black truck before, but couldn't place it. But I recognized Herman at once—his long, loping form, his smile, his warm brown eyes. There was another man with him, and Herman was carrying something that looked like a pie. It was not a pie, and it was not, as I'd assumed, sent by his wife. It was a peach kuchen baked by Herman from his late mother's recipe.

We chatted at my kitchen table for an hour over coffee and kuchen, and before Herman headed up the hill with his friend, I asked him for the recipe. It arrived in the mail a few days later, and thus began a correspondence that became the rich center of a mostly long-distance friendship.

Over time we came to understand that father and son traveled from their separate homes in their separate vehicles—100 miles for Herman, 180 for Ernie—to meet at the top of the hill. With parts of the roadway frequently impassible, they usually parked at a designated spot along the road and hauled their provisions up on foot. The farmhouse offered no physical comforts beyond a roof, a hearth, and half a dozen sagging beds that had been raided for nesting stuffs by a long lineage of mice. But it was so evident that this house provided something more essential than indoor plumbing or central heat or electric light, that it never occurred to me to wonder what that something was. At the very least, it was here, on this land that no longer provided a daily or seasonal base for anyone's life, but had come to be a convenient point of triangulation, that father and son had found their best opportunity to spend time together. We never met Ernie's older son, Ernst, Jr. He lived with his family next door to his widowed father, and saw him every day. He hadn't been to the farm in years.

It soon became a dream of mine, though I never said so, to walk these woods with Ernie—a great, gentle Paul Bunyan of a man with huge gnarled hands, quick to remove his cap when speaking to a lady

—and learn even an hour's worth of the many forest secrets I was sure he knew. As it happened, though, it was Herman who came to the farm more often, and who sometimes had the energy to venture down the hill at night to visit with us while his father slept after a full day of the heavy outdoor chores both men relished.

One didn't need much time with Herman to see that he loved the old place here with the particular sweet, enduring love inspired by happy memories of childhood. But there was more. His untrammeled pleasure in it had threaded through adolescence into adulthood, a fine motif that disappeared for long periods in the geographical complexities of his former military life, but always reemerged intact. The farm was close enough to some of the military bases where Herman had worked or studied that, from time to time, he'd used weekend leave to come here to relax or write a term paper. It had been a place for solitude and reflection—but also the opposite. Herman was a student of systems theory who nonetheless enjoyed such nineteenth century pursuits as writing letters by hand, sometimes enclosing a few lines of poetry he'd copied out from a favorite book, and sending them via the post office. He also liked to season his speech with a dash of his family's ancestral German, and he called the farm a *treffpunkt*, a meeting point, where friends and relatives from far and wide would gather for a few days with trucks and tents and coolers and children, to enjoy the challenge of camping out and share conversation, memories, target practice, campfires and spooky stories.

Still, Herman was absolutely clear-eyed about the economics of maintaining the old place, which the family seldom visited now. He and his wife, Diane, lived in a serene rural home surrounded by woods and fields busy with wildlife. Other family members no longer came to the farm. And the taxes on the two hundred acres kept going up, as taxes do. Most of all, Herman was increasingly concerned, as his father approached his eightieth year, that something be done to make sure that the farm's future would be determined by choice, rather than under duress.

"Change is a part of life," Herman would say, complaining about Ernie's resistance to making changes. Eventually, though, the old surveyor came and surveyed his beloved land anew, and with his son's help, marked the boundaries of a subdivision for official sanction. Some months later, we heard rumors that the subdivision had been approved, and the place was up for sale. We asked Herman about it, and to our surprise, he said he'd heard this from his brother, but that when he asked his father, Ernie was vague. Then one August morning a road crew churned past our house. Curiosity soon pressed us to follow them up the hill. Half way up, we met Ernie, alone here this time, with his cap and transit and a roll of red plastic tape. He was planning, he told us, though it wasn't settled yet, for some selective logging to be done. To facilitate this, he was having the road resurfaced with fresh dirt and rocks all the way to the top. He assured us that he was keeping a tight rein on things, and that the cutting would be limited to trees fifty to one hundred feet into the woods; there would be no visual impact on the road's character.

We invited him to join us for dinner that night, but he declined. He did, however, drop in the next afternoon on his way "down below," as local folk call Albany (a scant two hours away) and points south, suggesting to my ear Patagonia, Tierra del Fuego, Antarctica. Bob wasn't home, but I happened to be having coffee with our upstream neighbor, Betty. Though Ernie held title to the part of the stream that flowed past the house in which Betty and her husband had retired seven years ago, she and Ernie had never met. So the old gentleman sat and took a cup with us and had a slice of cake. Oh, yes, he always made the drive alone, he said. But he'd be eighty next spring, and after that, he added firmly, without a hint of sentiment, he wouldn't travel anymore.

"On Friday, October 28th, I met my Dad on the old farm road for an overnight visit...," Herman wrote us some weeks later, when we were back in Manhattan. "We met with a local logger, Mr. R. After nearly twenty years of discussion, my father and R. came to an agreement to begin some selective logging. My father is very concerned about the destruction of trees and long-term harm to the property, but he seems to have confidence in R.'s abilities and plan of action. We all know that there is no such thing as immaculate or faultless logging, however, selective cuttings will improve the forest in the long term."

About a week later, on a bright, warm Saturday at the top of the hill, we encountered a pleasant-looking young man riding around in a shiny truck with his two teenage sons. He introduced himself as the logger Ernie had engaged.

"It's better for the forest," Mr. R told us. "It looks better. You don't cut it, it's just going to rot." Then came the inevitable conversation about "good" trees and "bad" trees. We'd been startled to learn, as we settled into our cabin, that balsam firs, whose shapely spires and evocative aroma had drawn us to the neighborhood, and which some people prize for cabin-building because of their straightness, were considered "bad" trees here. They fall on their own after a relatively short life. In the regional economy, they are valued for neither timber nor pulp. Some of the saltier folk like Jim referred to them as nuisance trees, in a tone more hostile than merely dismissive, usually reserved for black flies. In the Northern Europe of our neighbors' forebears, the fir has been regarded as a tree of immortality since the middle ages; apparently this had passed from the cultural intelligence some generations back.

In any case, it was predictable that the logger who stood before us had no use for the balsams. But oh, how he craved the huge white pines in front of the farmhouse. He pointed out how the roof had worn away, the siding rotted as a result of their close shade. "Those trees should have gone years ago," he asserted.

Ernie Martin, however, had said "Absolutely not. You go in here under one condition: you don't touch any big pines." Mr. R told us that the old man had walked through each of his several hundred acres, indicating which trees could be cut. I could readily picture him doing this: bent but powerful, giving the bark a gentle pat with one of his massive hands.

Ernie Martin knows these woods, we agreed. He went to ranger school in Wanakena, we pointed out, just for something to say, unintentionally making the logger defensive enough to mention his own college degree. "Everyone thinks loggers are assholes," he added. "And there's some who give us a bad name, no doubt about that. But we're not all stupid, we're not a bunch of jerks."

We were somewhat reassured by this conversation. Much later, we realized we were being politicked. As we had prejudged him, he had stereotyped us, not fooled by our bright plaid shirts, our shapeless trousers and muddy boots, or by the fact that I nodded pleasantly and Bob made agreeable noises in response to everything he said. He knew we took an inimical view of his means of livelihood, whether he labeled us tree-huggers or merely flatlanders.

But folks of most persuasions along the spectrum of local ecopolitics, now that Ernie Martin and the old farm had come to their attention, were saying how foolish it was that Ernie hadn't logged years ago. They were saying, some even in so many words, that he'd been wasteful, letting good trees go to rot. Wasteful? I wondered. By permitting the natural cycles of life and death to manage his land? By failing to turn a forest into a commodity? Impressed by what Ernie had belatedly undertaken, two other landowners, infrequent visitors along the road, decided to follow suit. Both properties were in sight of ours.

7

On an anomalously spring-like Saturday in late January, we ventured up to the farm. We hadn't been to the top of the hill since our autumn encounter with the logger. It was a rare winter day. The sky had an intense blue clarity. The sun was strong, yet the temperature was cool enough to keep last night's snowfall intact. The woods were silent, and even as we trudged up the hill through fresh ruts ground into the roadway by the weight of logging trucks, we expected to find a place at the top where ours would be the first footprints in new snow.

A few days earlier, Herman had written:

"I haven't been over to the old farm road since we saw you there in early December. My father advises me that the loggers continue to work in the upper reaches of the property. He hasn't been up either, but seems content with the reports from R."

"…By the way, the Balsam sachet [you gave us] has had a remarkable life in our car. For some reason, the aroma seems to ascend at random times. For several weeks, we forgot the sachet was present until one day when the aroma reappeared. It is a pleasant reminder of the road…."

Long before I'd met the Martins, the old farm had taken on an independent life in my mind. At the bottom of the hill, or in New York City, I'd find myself thinking from time to time about how things were up there. Even after I knew its owners, I always thought of the house as being there by itself, doing whatever it did alone or with its ghosts.

It was a house of memories. That they were not my own—indeed, forever locked away and secret from me—didn't matter. Perhaps what a place inspires us to imagine contributes as much to its emotional weight as does its reality.

As the farmhouse had been an anchor point for me and Bob, bumbling, lost, in the woods, it remained fixed in my psyche—a place to which, in reality as well as in mind, I felt compelled to return. Going up the hill had become a kind of pilgrimage. We were attracted to the hilltop and to the house that marked it as to the center of a magnetic field. So I had by now accrued some small memories of it on my own. My recollections consisted primarily of moments of arrival. No matter what effort it took to get there—and in winter, it could be considerable—we never stayed long. Just to see it was enough.

The farmhouse was my first destination on cross-country skis, a thrilling accomplishment for someone whose muscles grow rigid at the slightest sensation of sliding underfoot, and who has never been able to tolerate the motion of skating or riding a bike. The following winter, there was a twilight walk in deep snow with a group of friends. Ours were the first footsteps in a fifteen-inch crust. We made our way down the glimmering hill in the dark.

Each visit affirmed the impressions of the last: that the house seemed happy enough to be by itself, emanated no wistfulness, regret, nostalgia, no hint of longing for the human life that once flung open its windows to breathe and give it breath. *Someone would come back.* Meanwhile, apparently unviolated by man or nature, it stood serene in its solitude.

Solitude. Serenity. As I observed these moods over time, the house became for me what Bachelard calls "one of those primal images that give us back areas of being," and suggest to us that "by living... in images that are as stabilizing as these are, we could start a new life, a life that would be our own, that would belong to us in our very depths."

We were near the top of the road when we heard the chain saws. The loggers were in the woods. Wind had deflected the sound. They'd been through the farm. My stunned eyes took in random details in chaotic sequence: mud, splintered trunks, shattered limbs akimbo, bark ground to pulp. All darkened the snow. Like a lover's betrayal, the devastation pulsed through my veins. The green and white vista my mind's eye had painted under the afternoon sun was all brown. And there was a smell, at once a green smell and a death smell. Fresh and alive, acrid and foul. Not a winter smell, not the smell of any season. Redolent of raw green wounds and decay. I imagined the other creatures of the woods, their olfactory powers immeasurably superior to mine, driven by their noses to flee for parts unknown, uprooted as the trees. Skinny bears stirring in their dens, birds scattering into the sky, chipmunks startled from their subterranean sleep to find the world changed…. And how their tunneled nests must rumble! Rabbits, their secret trails obliterated, fox, coyote, weasel, deer terrorized by the scent or the noise, or both. The familiar surely turned strange, too, for smaller creatures—toads and salamanders, insects busy in an unseen universe.

The road no longer ended at the farmhouse. It spread new fingers every which way.

Numbly, I followed Bob past the house toward the barn in the direction opposite the chain saws' sounds, on what had always been, at least in our acquaintance with the farm, a wide path mowed through an abandoned field. We stumbled through mud stuck with slippery limbs fresh-hacked, sharing for a moment the silent expectation that we'd soon reach an edge of untouched forest. But before we had got past the barn, we could see the chaos, on and on through the sparse, mangled, rakish standing trees.

We left quickly.

Unlike Bob, I took it personally.

"It's not your place," Bob said.

This was inarguable. Yet the feeling that something had been torn from me persisted. Vaguely embarrassed, I tried to cast off this shadow of loss, one I surely had no right to wear. The effort deepened my sorrow. By the time we'd reached the bottom of the hill, the object of my grief had taken a human form: I'd gone to visit an old friend only to discover his mutilated and dismembered corpse. Murdered in my absence. Defenseless and alone. Who was this friend? I wondered. I had personified the forest around the old farmhouse as male, elderly, trusting, a little frail, but independent and, as I'd fancied the house, content in a treasured solitude. Couldn't I have protected him somehow?

It was my impulse to phone Herman at once. Surely this would not be happening if he knew about it. Well, maybe it would. This was, Herman had made clear, strictly Ernie's affair, and one in which neither Herman nor his brother was routinely consulted or even informed. I guessed that Ernie Martin had changed his mind about saving the old pines. Or the loggers simply took the trees they coveted. With the trees gone, there was nothing to be done. Neither legal recourse nor raw revenge can restore a tree cut in error, carelessness or greed.

Nonetheless, that evening, I wrote Herman an unreservedly emotional letter. I showed it to Bob, and he urged me not to send it. Once I'd hesitated, it seemed increasingly less likely I was offering information Herman did not know. I returned to the city with the letter folded into the back of my journal.

But as I went about my urban life, I was haunted by two things. First, the "friend" I'd failed. Who was he, this elder for whom I felt not only respect and affection, but also a profound sense of duty? Not Ernie. I didn't know him well enough. Surely not my father, whom I didn't regard as elderly, nor either of my late grandfathers. His identity remained elusive. Bob, who had spent some time in Brazil before I met him, said my mysterious elder reminded him of Caboclo, an ancestral male figure of Brazilian tribal religion who embodies the spirit of the forest.

And indeed, the second thing that preoccupied me was only in part about the violence to what I'd seen and begun to understand. More troubling, what would become of all the myriad aspects of the forest's life that I had never encountered and now, never would? It occurred to me that I didn't know the smallest fraction of what was there, but I was sure that after the logging there was much less of it. I mourned all the animals and plants I never saw because they're far too small or because I didn't look hard enough or never chanced on the right intersection of light and time and place.

Scat near my house and claw marks on the farm's old apple trees told of bears afoot, but I'd never seen one. Nor had I seen an owl here, though I'd heard many. These are the common creatures of this place, the creatures to whom it belonged before humans came, and which, days or weeks ago, probably outnumbered us in these few square miles. I wondered, too, about the rare—the moose whose unmistakably huge tracks had plummeted across our hillside last winter, the indigo bunting with unearthly blue feathers that had once—only once—shimmered by like a mirage. Some things I might eventually have come to know, the way I'd discovered a field of pink lady's slippers on our land in a serendipitous shift of light as I walked past it for the hundredth or thousandth time. Others I could only imagine: a pair of bear cubs tumbling from the den on the first warm day of March, a great horned owl swooping nestward. Still others, their lives disrupted in ways too many and large and subtle for me to fathom are invisible to me by their very nature and mine: insect societies; a universe of microscopic fungi as unexplored as those of the tropics; the 10,000 species of bacteria, most as yet unidentified, that inhabit a single gram of northeastern forest soil.

Bob and I are both preoccupied in very different ways with things not visible to the naked eye. Binoculars, cameras, lenses, were among our first gifts to each other as we shared new ways of looking at the physical world. Bob is an amateur photographer whose favorite subjects are the tiniest of flowers and the most distant of galaxies. With his ongoing involvement with the sky's vast and remote objects, he is increasingly fascinated with things tiny and near: lichen, molecules, microbes. As a writer, my strongest inclinations are to bring to the page the inner life, my own and that of real and imagined others: emotions, and sometimes dreams, which are essentially visual, albeit invisible to the day's eye.

The forest is, in large part, an unseen universe. I asked myself how much I really cared about this invisible world beneath my world. Not as much, I had to admit as I care about the larger creatures I know to have some concept of home. But I know, too, that the integrity of their homes can be profoundly threatened by events in the universe of the too-small-to-care-about, just as the activities of carpenter ants threaten mine. It did not occur to me to include in my mental forest community the loggers themselves, who were also my neighbors, and who, like their fathers or grandfathers or uncles before them, fed their families by cutting trees. Nor did I think, then, about what ultimately becomes of those trees: Construction lumber? Firewood? Furniture? Writing paper, books, toilet tissue? I use all of these, as I eat meat and wear leather.

In the end, I held my letter to Herman for two weeks, added a long caveat about honesty, conflict and friendship, and put it in the mail. Herman replied,

> I have mixed emotions regarding the logging and the loss of the old pines. I have not seen the farm…so my comments are based on your account and my observations prior to the cutting. For several years my Dad and I have looked at the old pines and several of the other large trees around the house. We were a bit concerned about their proximity to the building and we were fortunate that several large branches fell away

from the house during storms. Thus, the decision to take down the old pines was done to ensure the structure remains. Believe me, we both liked the old pines but it was recognized that they must go as a pair. They were a genuine team—extending their welcome and shelter. Once felled, R. told my father, the interior of the pines revealed deterioration far worse than the exterior displayed.

When I visit the farm, I'm sure to experience the grief, the shock and perhaps guilt/regret over the decision made. I'll look to the younger pines for strength as they begin their role of shelter, beauty, and extending a welcome to hikers, hunters and wildlife.

Well, I'll leave you with this excerpt from Emerson. Perhaps you will find some comfort in his words:

> *It is time to be old,*
> *To take in sail:*
> *The god of bounds,*
> *Who sets to seas ashore,*
> *Came to me in his fatal rounds,*
> *And said: 'No more!*
> *No farther shoot*
> *Thy broad ambitious branches, and thy root…*
> *There's not enough for this or that,*
> *Make thy option which of two;*
> *Economize the failing river…*
> *Leave the many and hold the few.'*

8

When Herman's letter reached me, nearly a month had passed since our January walk up the hill. Still, I could barely see the reason in his words. My relief that Herman hadn't taken offense barely tempered my disappointment that he didn't feel the same sense of loss about what was happening to his property as I did.

My mind scarcely registered the plain fact he stressed: the pines I mourned were at the end of their lives and could have fallen on the house. As for the Emerson poem, jarred by its first line, I skimmed it so hastily I failed to comprehend its obvious point. Taking the words "It's time to grow old" to refer to myself, I misread it altogether. I didn't think it was time yet for me to grow old, so I was—fleetingly—perplexed and a little annoyed that Herman had copied this out for me.

I put the letter aside with the sense that the values Bob and I shared might diverge more significantly from our neighbor's than we'd believed. Bob didn't give any of this much thought. I, on the other hand, felt a twinge of betrayal. But I soon stepped away from this feeling. Herman and I came from such different worlds, I regarded our friendship as something of a miracle. One dissonant note was hardly surprising. I chalked it off to the inevitable country/city dichotomy that sooner or later colored virtually all of our relationships here. It was a difference in viewpoint, and often in opinion, that didn't taint the growing affection, graciously reciprocated, that we felt for our closest neighbors, indeed, for most everyone in the community with whom we had a more than a passing acquaintance. Hunters/non-hunters, pro-loggers/anti-loggers—these differences were difficult, but we'd learned they could be managed.

Nonetheless, my first impression reasserted itself: the logging of the farm was a disaster. I grew increasingly curious to know how Herman, and especially Ernie, would feel when they saw the result of what in theory, I began to understand, had been a reasonable plan. Surely this wasn't the "good job" of logging they'd expected, without impact on the visual character of the road, or on the most venerable trees. I hoped and more than half believed that once Ernie saw what had happened thus far to his woods he'd stop it before it got any worse.

I never had the opportunity to ask Ernie how he felt about what had become of his land, or even to gauge his response. On a Friday afternoon in late March, shortly before Easter, his car partly packed for the 180-mile drive up to see, finally, what the loggers had done, great, vigorous Ernie, dressed for the journey in boots and parka, fell to his kitchen floor. Within moments or hours—no one knows for sure—he was dead of a stroke.

Herman phoned us in Manhattan the next morning with the news. And he told Bob, who took the call, that he'd spoken to Mr. R. and instructed him to halt all logging until further notice. I wanted to go to the funeral, some 80 miles upstate, but I was grounded with my hip fracture. We wired flowers.

A few weeks later, Herman included with one of his letters a copy of the Reverend Susan Zink's eulogy for his beloved father. The Martin men weren't churchgoers, and the Reverend had never met Ernie. But on the basis of a long talk with his older son, Ernst, Jr., she took for her theme Ernst Sr.'s lifelong love of trees.

"…Ernst Martin left memories behind rooted in the soil, destined for growth, one with the earth. His Easters included a trek into the woods to plant evergreens, with his sons plodding along.

"Besides planting trees to better the earth, Ernst planted memories in the hearts of those around him to better their lives. And with trees, you'd have to include in that number those who haven't been born yet. Thomas Fuller knew about this kind of person when he observed: 'He that plants trees loves others beside himself.…'

"Look around you and see the moonlight framing one of his Easter gifts to you. Listen and hear the winds moving through the needles. Take a deep breath and smell the fragrance of the pine…."

Reverend Zink went on to say that Ernie liked to use tree metaphors when making a point, thus linking him with Jesus, whom she described as "a great observer of trees." After pointing out the significance of the Tree of Life as a symbol for heaven, she concluded: "What a picture. Ernst headed for the woods, bending down, hands in the dirt, his memories left behind, rooted in your hearts, destined for growth, one with the earth."

Herman was pleased with the eulogy, and thought it a fitting farewell. But, despite my fondness for Herman and my feeling for his loss, I felt stung by the ironies innocently hidden there. If the Reverend's words truly described Ernie, how could he do this to his trees? There was something I was not understanding.

It was, as I was eventually to learn, quite simple: back taxes were owed, and if they weren't paid, the property would be lost. The trees had been sold off to pay this debt. And, after a brief hiatus following Ernie's death, the logging was resumed. Having inspected the land himself, Herman assured me the loggers had done a good job. I took his word for it. But I couldn't imagine—if this was good—what was bad?

And there was no way that anyone, not even Ernie or Herman, could have predicted that the decision to log on the old farm would trigger a chain reaction.

One Saturday the previous fall, a few weeks after our conversation with Mr. R. in the forest, when the logging of the Martin property had just begun, I'd walked to the edge of my driveway, as I routinely did in early morning, just to look around. Two men I'd never seen before were coming toward me out of the woods on a path directly across the road. They were walking about forty feet apart, carrying a long tape measure between them. I said good morning. They just nodded.

Clearly they weren't going to identify themselves or tell me what they were doing, and I went about my business. But from the vegetable patch I was turning over, I overheard snatches of their conversation. They were measuring distances from the stream.

How close to a stream can you log?

Or build?

Since there was no vehicle parked on the road, they'd got into the woods some other way. There was no structure on the land, a sizeable piece that had access from the main road. It was privately owned, by people no one seemed to know. We'd heard they lived in Pennsylvania, but then we heard a lot of things. Were these the owners? Or were they loggers?

Bob came out and we walked back to the road together. The men were gone without a trace, as if they'd never been there.

I never did find out who they were, or account for their unfriendliness, as anomalous in this community as a bear in Rockefeller Center. And no timber was taken from the vicinity of the stream. But some selective cutting did take place. Each time we visited our cabin over the winter, we observed that the dense conifers across the road had grown more sparse. In their place, I pictured the imminent appearance of driveways and eventually houses and traffic.

Back in the city, I dreamed of walking to the end of my driveway, just as I had that fall morning, to discover that a MacDonald's had been erected on the spot.

Bob, too, had his nightmares, this one perhaps triggered by the sound of a pre-dawn snowplow as we slept one winter morning in the cabin.

"There was heavy equipment. Seven-foot chain saws attached to trucks were ripping down our trees," Bob related. "It was like a clearcut in a tropical rain forest. The earth was all red and brown. The rest of the road had turned into a fifties' amusement park, with penny arcades. The whole road was widened, and there were no woods. Ours was the only wooded part of the road left, and now they were tearing the trees down."

We were waiting, as it were, for the next tree to drop. And it did —but from a different direction.

The trees I hear falling on this beautiful spring day, a few weeks after Ernie Martin's funeral, are not across the road, nor are they the Martin family's trees. They are the trees of our neighbor, Duane, just across the stream.

Now, Bob, too, is appalled. "I hate to do this to you," he says. "But you have to see this." On crutches, I make my way slowly through the spring sunshine toward the edge of the lawn, into the shade of the great spruce where Bob is standing, and look across the water.

When we'd first seen our cabin and pondered the weathered old picnic table nestled among the pristine evergreens across the stream, the real estate agent told us that small property belonged to a quiet family with three teenage daughters, and that they used the place for only two weeks each year. It wasn't until the day of the closing that we learned no such family had ever owned it, and that it currently belonged to a young single man named Duane. Duane did have a daughter. She was two.

Though we'd had other unforeseen problems from across the water, despite our concerns about the table, we'd never been aware of anyone picnicking or so much as parking a beer on it. Nor had anyone jumped into the water from the opposite shore for more than a second's dip, followed by a scream and retreat, quick and final, back into the forest that hid Duane's small red clapboard cabin from the shore.

But now, when I reach the spruce tree where Bob is waiting for me, I see that the familiar curtain of trees across the stream is gone. Trunks are half-skewed, appendages severed, limbs hacked to bones, the forest butchered. And there is Duane's house, no longer a little cabin, but a tall, square two-story affair in the middle of a renovation interrupted a year ago, no siding on it, the silvery face of its naked insulation angled toward us, shining in the sun.

The trees I'd heard falling were the trees that grew at the very edge of the stream—all of them. Nothing was left on the bank but a few pathetic stragglers—a bit of alder, a couple of half-dead maples that had been partially uprooted in a storm.

Bob helps me back to my chair and goes for a walk. He returns to report that Duane's skinless house is visible from every point along the stream, and every high spot on our rolling land.

"I'm going over there," Bob says.

He learns that the logging is finished except for some cleanup. Duane is not there and not expected. But even the loggers are puzzled by why he'd wanted to take down all he'd instructed them to cut.

I recall a brief conversation I had with Duane last fall, moments after I'd seen the two men with the tape measure across the road. The sun had come over the low hemlocks that stood between our garden and the stream. Duane and I were standing quietly for a moment, just basking in the beautiful morning. Then Duane looked over toward his place and said he planned to talk to Mr. R., since all the heavy equipment was already here, about taking down a couple of his big pines near the bridge. "I got to check with the DEC, first though," he said. "They can fine you a thousand bucks an inch if you cut something you're not supposed to."

The hollow space where alarm resides fell open in the pit of my stomach, but it quickly sealed itself up again. The pines he pointed to faced the end of our property, near the road, and had no impact on our privacy. Besides, I was sure the Department of Environmental Conservation would say no, and that would be the end of it.

We'd known for a long time that Duane's plan for his house included the addition of a living room to the current structure, with a big deck facing the stream, and that he'd want to thin some trees to get himself a view. But not only had Duane run out of money for his renovation, most of which he'd done himself with the help of friends, but his well was failing. He had to scrape together thousands to drill a new one to supply the dishwasher and washing machine and Jacuzzi, to say nothing of the sinks and toilets, before he did anything else. So we figured we'd worry about those trees when the deck started to go up, if it ever did. The view Duane wanted could have been carved out easily without butchery.

Instead, Duane has clearcut all the way to the stream. *Tabula rasa.*

The logger had told Bob that he and his crew had repeatedly questioned Duane's decision. I can hear them saying, "You sure you want that cut?" rather like a barber facing an elegant head of thick silvery locks on a client who has requested a buzz cut and a dye job of electric blue. Even the loggers think it looks like a war zone.

And in our first moments of rage and loss, war is what we plan to undertake. This is the Adirondacks. We have laws against such things.

The trees I'd heard falling were trees we thought could never be cut because they grew within the boundaries of the largest park in the US, bigger than some small states in their entirety. It was here, more than one hundred years ago, that the ravages of excessive logging inspired the east's famous first foray into conservation laws.

In the days that followed, however, we learned that we were misinformed about the particulars of these laws.

How close to a stream can you log? Or build?

I had conflated the answers to these two questions, a common confusion in a state park of which the state owns only 43 percent. The Adirondack Forest Preserve may be America's best-protected public wildlands. But these lands are interspersed with more than three million acres of private holdings ranging from tiny specks to towns and hamlets, huge nineteenth century retreats built and still held by wealth and power, and vast parcels of paper company forest.

Numerous regulations do limit use of private lands here, as zoning laws and building codes do everywhere. My mind clung to a passage from a book I'd read a decade ago, in which a woman described building herself a log cabin on the shore of a remote Adirondack lake, only to be served with a summons for violating a covenant stating that no structure could be erected within fifty feet of the shore. Hers was thirty-eight feet. She was given ninety days or so to tear down the cabin, move it twelve feet, or face a lawsuit. She moved it.

I was sure Duane had broken the law by cutting the trees at the water's edge because those trees were a hundred feet closer to the stream than our cabin, and we'd been told many times that the law would never permit the construction of a dwelling so close to the water today. And over the years, I'd talked to several people with waterfront homes who were struggling to strike a balance between an ideal view, environmental values, and the law.

But logging, we learned after a flurry of official consultations, is not governed by the same rules as building, and lakes and ponds are sometimes regulated differently than rivers and streams. There is essentially one rule about logging on private land along a stream like ours within the Adirondack Park: as long as the bank is not sufficiently eroded to silt the water and compromise its quality, you can cut anything you please, right to the water's edge.

I cursed my broken hip. We'd planned to be here four days earlier, but had delayed the trip on doctor's orders. If we'd known Duane's plan we might have implored him to reconsider what remained of his trees. Yes, he needed money. Still, I think perhaps we would have been persuasive enough to rescue some of them.

I held this notion even though there was no logic, but rather something violent and irrational about what Duane had done. Upsetting as the Martins' logging was to me, the logging on Duane's place seemed by comparison an act of rage, characterized by the tortured brutality of self-mutilation, like cutting off a nose to spite a face, like van Gogh slicing off his ear.

Instead of looking out on a lovely forest from his house, Duane looked down toward the stream across a slope of hacked-off limbs. He never cleaned up any of the debris left by the loggers, nor for nearly a year did he even visit his house to enjoy the view he had created for himself from the room yet to be built. Month by month, storm by storm, all the stragglers toppled, too, adding their corpses to the pile.

We weren't the only people who were upset about what came to be known around the neighborhood as Duane's debacle. Bob was the first to use the phrase, and it stuck.

Everyone else who came to the road—including Herman—gaped at what they saw across the stream, and asked, "Why on earth did he do that?"

I scarcely knew Duane, but I thought I knew why.

PART IV

Old Man of the Forest

*The more our lives move off the beaten
track, the fewer road signs we will encounter.
Finally, we end up in the very bush of our
lives, a place where we have to navigate
purely on an inner sense of direction as we
are daily confronted with new terrain....*

*The entire habitual psychological system is
geared toward steering clear of the unknown,
even when we have the intention to face what
we know not.*

Tracks in the Wilderness of Dreaming,
Robert Bosnak

9

Ernie Martin's death was the second loss to come to the old farm road within six months. The first was our nearest neighbor, Jim, whose house was on the other side of the bridge, cater-corner to ours.

Jim was the road's lone full-time resident and all of us some-timers —four households in all—made a point of telling him what we were up to. Not that he ever asked. But he noted who came and went—all who belonged here and those who didn't—and always kept burning in his window a bright light anyone could see before crossing the bridge, a light that stood sentry over the road like a bridge troll.

The real estate agent had told us Jim would be a wonderful neigh-bor (this proved to be the one thing about which he spoke the truth) and once we'd begun negotiations to purchase the cabin, we were eager to meet him.

Over the next few months, we visited the road as often as we could to see how it wore the changing season. Each time, we tentatively walked up Jim's short driveway and mounted the three or four steps to the unfinished wood stoop at the front door. The big, dormered brown A-frame, more roof than house at first glance, always gave the impression that someone was home. But no one was. Unaccustomed to knocking on strangers' doors, we felt like trespassers, left quickly. We didn't take in many particulars about the place, but it seemed to be a work-in-progress, to judge from the piles of lumber and other building supplies in the yard. So when I asked the real estate agent what Jim did, meaning, what was his job, I was surprised when the man said, "I don't know. I believe he's retired." I'd pictured mysterious Jim as someone in his late twenties or early thirties. The house had struck me as young man's house, the home of a busy person with lots of energy. This last part, at least, was correct.

The second time we knocked at Jim's door, there were several large black garbage bags in the driveway. There's no trash pickup in these sparsely populated northern counties, and everyone knows leaving stuff like this around is a foolish invitation to raccoons, porcupines, bears. I assumed he'd be right back. We waited a bit, but Jim didn't appear. When we returned a few weeks later, the bags were still there: ripped asunder by some curious animal, they'd spilled their contents of soda bottles and other recyclables onto the dirt. Naively, I wondered if Jim had been called out of town suddenly, or perhaps was ill, even in the hospital. I created a story: he'd brought these bags outside to take them to the dump, or redeem the bottles for the nickel deposit at some store, but before he'd been able to do so, something important had called him away. On a subsequent visit, we found things more or less the same. Still, this was the only way I could explain to myself how "a wonderful neighbor" could have left this mess in his driveway. It was not the right explanation.

On the morning of closing, we met the agent at the cabin one last time, and when we'd completed our inspection, the three of us went across the road to try Jim again. This time, the door was opened by a rather tall elderly man with brilliant blue eyes and a big smile. Looking into those direct, merry eyes as I shook his firm hand, I liked and trusted him at once. While we chatted, he reached into his shirt pocket and withdrew a few peanuts to feed the chipmunk that had come scampering up the stoop. The creature climbed his leg as if he were a tree and, with Jim's encouragement, made it all the way to his shirt pocket, into which it crawled and ate the rest of the peanuts from the shell.

Slender and unbowed by age, Jim had big hands and feet that seemed to belong on a body larger than his six-foot frame. And though his pate was shiny and his brow deeply creased, his meaty, capable-looking hands were smooth. The wide, gold wedding band on his ring finger drew my attention to these hands that seemed a decade or so younger than the rest of him, as if they lived a separate life. Did widowers wear wedding bands? No one had mentioned a wife.

Jim watched our cabin through the ten months of the year when we were mostly in the city, made sure the town plowed our driveway, and when he thought they hadn't done a proper job, went over it himself with an old plow attached to a rusty, unregistered brown truck he'd recently towed down from Eleventh Mountain. He shoveled a path to our door, and turned on the heat when we phoned ahead, so that even on subzero nights we arrived at a warm house. Payment for these invaluable services was out of the question, though gourmet treats from Manhattan and home-cooked meals were graciously accepted. He did the same for Duane, and when the young man began to transform his cabin into a two-story house, Jim worked side by side with him and the friends he brought from "down below" each weekend, and oversaw deliveries and work done in Duane's absence.

On the rare occasions when the Martins or their friends planned a trip to the farm, Jim would drive as far up the hill as the rusty truck would go before things got too muddy or rutted, and though all Ernie ever asked him to do was take a look and let him know how far up they could expect to drive, Jim always took his ax and chain saw and cleared any fallen trees.

The fourth household on the road was a little hunting camp, the landmark that had told us we were finally home after our night in the forest. Jim opened this place, too, for the perennially absent owner's various friends, most of whom were firemen from "down below." In the fall, a party of hunters would come and stay for several weeks. They rewarded Jim with venison and whatever supplies remained at the end of their trip, and Jim described these handouts in loving detail, from the weight and quality of the fresh meat down to the last can of beans, as if they were a king's ransom. Then he rambled into tales of venison feasts from "the old days" when the camp's owner hunted there, descriptions of meals that seemed so long past they might have been consumed in King Arthur's forest.

Eventually, I realized that it was the presence in these older stories of Jim's wife, Helen, that gave them their remote, nostalgic tone. It wasn't that Helen didn't often figure in Jim's yarns. He talked about her all the time. But the narratives in which she appeared tended to be set in the recent past in Burlington, Vermont, where she still lived, or in Jim's pre-retirement Pleistocene just about anywhere in the world his extensive business travels had taken them. We understood that Helen hadn't been seen on this road for some years.

She didn't like it here, Jim said. She was allergic to the mosquitoes and black flies in the summer, and the winters were too cold.

"Now, when I get the house finished…but the upstairs isn't done, and the way it is, she isn't really comfortable," Jim told us. "She likes things just so. Can't get used to all my projects and things I've got going." And she had a job, some kind of social work for the county. Since he'd had his heart attacks, Jim explained, life in Burlington was "too much activity" for him: the hustle of the city (population 30,000, as compared to the 300 in our hamlet) and the busyness of the two-family house Helen shared with her daughter and three small grandchildren. Nope, too much excitement. Wasn't good for him.

Jim was proud of the good health he'd enjoyed for many years since the heart trouble, and he attributed it in part to the way he'd apportioned off his days and weeks into appointed rounds. He had his routines, he explained, didn't change them for anything. If Thursday was his bingo night in Glens Falls, he'd be there, barring anything but a blizzard, even if it meant turning down a dinner invite or paying work.

Jim visited his wife every Friday, usually beginning the two-hour drive at 6 a.m. and returning well after dark. He talked of breakfasts in Port Henry, lunch in Burlington, rarely referred to dinner, and never spent the night. Yet the Burlington house remained Jim's residence of record. Vermont was the state of his birth, and to the disdain of many of his Adirondack neighbors, who considered his green license plates a scandal, it was where he voted, registered his cars, and paid such taxes as he paid, even though, as we were eventually to learn, he hadn't spent a night there in more than a decade.

Every morning before 8, he was "in town," perched at the counter in the diner, where he had coffee and a homemade donut, and acquired local news and gossip from miles around. This he reported selectively, rarely passing on anything that reflected badly on anyone. Rarely did he volunteer negative opinions on any subject, though he expressed silent opposition to local environmental policies every day by wearing a cap with the logo "Adirondacks in the 21st Century" emblazoned above a cartoon dinosaur cavorting among giant ferns. Once in a great while, he'd lambaste some "liberal" ideas, claiming that acid rain didn't exist, and extolling the value of logging: "Good for the forest," he said. "Lets in the light." And he did have a way to let you know if he didn't like something—a long pause, a brief frown, a lift of his brow, an effort to make his face stern. But his specialty was praising the skills and talents of his friends—almost as lavishly as he praised his own—and offering such tidbits as, "It was 18 below at Strohmeyer's this morning," and high and low temperatures in various local places for the past 24 hours, as well as long range weather forecasts. In fact, for just about anything you wanted to know, down to when the berries would be ripe to whether it was a deer, a rabbit, or a woodchuck that had dined on your young spinach plants last night, Jim was more than happy to provide the answer.

Now, Jim would have known who those men with the tape measure were. Had he been home, he would have been out there chatting with them, and had he been away on one of his usual sorts of errands, he would have soon found out what they were up to. But on the afternoon of the fall day that began for me with the tape measure men at the end of our driveway, Bob and I saw Jim for the last time in a hospital room in Burlington. Ailing all summer, he'd finally seen a doctor just after Labor Day and been hospitalized at once.

It had been only a few weeks since Jim had left the road, but already his absence had changed the dynamics of the neighborhood: we'd begun to talk to Duane, and he to us, partly because of our shared concern for Jim, but also because, without Jim around, we had no choice.

As Jim had been our friend, Duane was our enemy—at least that was how we'd come to think of him.

Our first meeting with Duane was pleasant enough.

A Sunday evening, early twilight. After a month of settling into the cabin, we were entertaining our first weekend guests: a family of three in the loft, and in tents pitched in mossy clearings in the woods, my daughter, Elizabeth, just graduated from college, and our friend, Charles, a bassoonist who'd come to play duets with Bob.

This they were doing on the front lawn as the rest of us listened, spellbound. We were immersed in Beethoven's "Duo #1 for Bassoon and Clarinet" when Jim, accompanied by a shorter, rounder, younger man and a tiny girl, came across the bridge and tiptoed up our path. Duane and his daughter were discreetly introduced. I slipped into the house to get more beer.

There is something that never fails to thrill me in the music Bob and Charles play in the natural chamber of our small lawn, reverberating through the permeable walls of the forest, in counterpoint with the birds and the endless improvisations of the stream. These first moments are transcendent, the music at once utterly incongruous and sublimely congruent with the birds and the flowing water and the riffling of the mild, balsam-scented air. In the gently gathering dark, our neighbors' amiable faces were lit with a befuddled wonder. I guessed they were unfamiliar with such sounds, but happy enough to hear them. Even the child clinging to her father's hand—a beautiful toddler with soft chocolate eyes and a cap of dark, wavy hair—needed no prompting to be attentive. She was, as much as any of us, entranced by the music.

When the long duet was over, Bob apologized, in characteristic immodest modesty, for disturbing the peace. Duane welcomed us to the neighborhood, enumerated the many tools housed in his garage, invited us to make use of them, and, along with Jim, soon bid us good night.

Ok, we thought. This bodes well enough.

A still Sunday afternoon the following summer. Bob, engaged in a first crude attempt at making rustic furniture, is out front almost at the very spot where he and Charles had set their music stands— shaving down half a cedar log with a draw-knife. I'm prowling in the woods beyond the driveway, looking for shapely cedar branches on the ground. Whiz-bang! Bullets fly so close I jump. Bob is much closer to the sound, and I rush out of the woods through a tangle of brambles to make sure he's all right. The bullets keep coming, rapid to my uneducated ears as machine-gun fire.

We're not just annoyed. We're afraid. Do we call the police? What police? There's no local law enforcement here, not even a sheriff, only the state police barracks twenty miles north. Calling up there seems too extreme. Especially since we can't identify a law that's been broken. Surely not a game law: they can't be pumping so much ammo at anything alive. What are the rules about target practice? Bob, who earned an expert marksman's rating in the Army, identifies the firearm as a rifle by the sound. We're not about to go up the road to investigate; the bullets are flying so close we decide we're better off in the house. The shooting persists for hours, shredding the day. Even inside, the shots ring loud. Eventually, we get in the car and go off to take a hike and dine out in another town.

Over dinner, it occurred to us there was one thing we could do: talk to Jim. We knew Jim was fond of Duane, but he liked us, too.

A day or so later, when he strolled up our path, we asked, "Did you hear all that shooting on Sunday afternoon?" Nope. He was in Glens Falls all day and all evening.

"What's the law?"

"Five hundred feet. From a building or a road."

"Well, they were a damn sight closer than five hundred feet."

"I'll check into it."

The next day, Jim assured us he "gave 'em what for" and that it wouldn't happen again. "Some of 'em, they come for a couple days from down below, they don't know anything. Duane—he knows better. I told him, you can't do that. You maybe think you're out in the middle of nowhere, but there's other people here. You do anything stupid like that again, you answer to me."

Much later, we heard from the forest ranger who lives just upstream that, his infant's nap disrupted by the noise, he'd come to investigate and found Duane and friends had set up a picnic table in the middle of road and were shooting beer cans off it. He read them the riot act and issued a summons. If Jim knew about this, he never mentioned it.

Childish as it seems now to tell it, we got into the habit of communicating with Duane only through Jim. Had we encountered Duane by chance, we would have been cordial. But we never ran into him and we didn't seek him out. We rationalized that we were avoiding angry confrontations. More to the point, we didn't want to be tagged as city folks who felt our priorities were more worthy than those of people who'd come to these woods before we had. "You can't bring New York City here with you and expect everyone to change their ways," I'd heard a friend say about a young couple who'd moved to a nearby town and tried to make their mark on local politics. I didn't want this said of us.

And so it went. Fortuitously, Duane rarely spent more than the odd weekend here during the summer. He took his vacation time during hunting season, and then we simply stayed away—not a great hardship, since our fall schedules were tight. But when a summer's day exploded in hours of intermittent gunfire, we'd complain to Jim (as if he were the management) and Jim would relay the complaint to Duane. At the same time—sometimes in the same conversation—Jim related Duane's doings to us as if we were all mutual friends. We were treated to weekly updates on Duane's renovation. Every Monday or Tuesday, Jim insisted on unlocking Duane's place, where he provided guided tours to such attractions as the new kitchen cabinets and the wiring system, boasting of all that had been accomplished over the weekend and how well it had been done. Not that we wanted these tours, but it would have been rude to refuse. The modest cabin was being transformed into a suburban house with dishwasher, laundry room, sauna, Jacuzzi, air-conditioning. How long before Duane joined Jim on the road full-time? When that happened, we were resigned, our cabin would go up for sale.

Seasons passed, and though we occasionally heard Duane, we saw no more of him than his van crossing the bridge.

July 2, 1:30 a.m. We arrive from Manhattan for our summer stay, after six hours on the road. The preceding months have been rough, with the usual job stress compounded by painful health problems (shingles for Bob, debilitating migraines for me). Bob's teaching semester ended yesterday; I'd finished a grueling six-month editorial stint minutes before we hit the road. Opening the car doors, we hear an amplified guitar twanging above the rushing stream. Then something else. A chain saw? A lawn mower? At this hour? As we unpack the car, we try to place the vicious, ratcheting buzz. It crosses the bridge, proceeds along the edge of our property for a hundred yards or so, then turns around only to repeat the same routine a moment later. We approach with caution, peer out to the road between the trees. It's an ATV, a four-wheeled roadcruncher of a toy for grownups. We hope that by the time we empty the car and are ready for bed whoever is engaged in this repetitive pursuit will have tired of it. At 2:30 a.m. they have not.

Finally, we step out into the road and shine flashlights at the bridge so that anyone coming across will drive into their beams. Sure enough, riding straight into them—and almost into us, as if we weren't there —comes a drunken man we've never seen before, beer bottle in hand, hugely fat. He is hanging on to a female—a very small woman or large child—who is half in his lap, half dragging in the dust.

"Excuse me," Bob says mildly, "but it's two a.m. We'd like to get some sleep."

The fat man looks dazed and surprised that anyone else is there. That there is anyone else in the world. Another of these vehicles comes roaring up behind him, driven by someone who, although we aren't certain in the dark, appears to be Duane.

The ATVs turn tail and the night grows quiet. But they resume in the morning and continue all weekend. Across the bridge, along our property and back. Over and over again. Finally, Bob goes to Duane's house. Duane isn't there, but he asks the man who is if they wouldn't mind driving the other way, up toward the farm. Sure, no problem.

Later in the week: Did Jim know about this? Saturday night? No, he was asleep, didn't hear a thing. Sunday? Working all day in Glens Falls. Just came home to sleep.

Every weekend that summer there was a large contingent of people at Duane's house, hammering and sawing. Bob dubbed them *"Der Nibelungen"* after the anvil-pounding dwarves of Wagner's Ring Cycle. We ran into Duane once or twice, and each time he'd apologize for the noise, and we'd say, "no problem," which was true. It was the noise involving firearms or ATVs that was the problem. We begin to have revenge fantasies. My brother, who has a weakness for buying antique stereo equipment he doesn't need, had acquired an enormous set of speakers circa 1955, heavy on the bass. Should we hook them up and blast Wagnerian opera across the stream?

Our enmity with Duane was sealed one afternoon when I was alone, reading at our picnic table. I heard some activity from the vicinity of the stream. Before I could get up to peer through the shrubs, three shots were fired from the opposite shore. Clearing my throat and forcing a loud cough, I hurried the half dozen steps to the edge of the lawn. Two young men, strangers to me, were standing across the stream, rifles in hand, less than a hundred feet away.

"Hello," they said. "How ya doing?"

"I'd be doing a lot better if you weren't shooting at me," I replied.

"Oh, we're not shooting over there. We're just shooting into the woods."

I was now convinced that Duane was endangering our lives, not intentionally, but stupidly, by opening his house to people with guns who had no idea there were other people nearby, and no sense of where it was safe—or legal—to fire them.

When I spoke to Jim, I dropped all pretense of diplomacy. Even he was alarmed. "Them from down below, they don't know nothin'. Duane has to learn, even if he's not here, he's responsible for who is. If he don't understand that, I'll sure make him. He can't just hand over his keys and say go on, tear up the woods, do anything you want."

Whatever Jim said to Duane, and I'm sure he said something, it seemed unlikely to prevent future conflict between the very different and mutually exclusive ways of life for which we'd chosen this remote place. If it wasn't literally turf in dispute, it was a territorial battle nonetheless. Like birds, we each sought dominion over the airspace.

Now, with Jim in the hospital, Duane came onto our place for the first time I could recall since the Beethoven impromptu more than three years earlier.

It was that same gray Saturday morning, moments after I'd seen the strangers stretching their measuring tape between trees and stream on the other side of the road. As I pulled my dead tomato plants, I was mentally preparing myself to phone Jim at the hospital to find out what time we should visit. Looking out toward the road, I thought of the countless times I'd stood just like this in the early morning, listening for Jim's car the way I listened for the birds. And then I saw Duane coming up our path. His step was tentative, his expression a little abashed. But I was glad to see him.

"Have you been to the hospital?" I asked. He had. Yesterday, he'd skipped a half day of work to travel from New Jersey to Vermont in time to spend the evening with Jim.

"I'm on my way back there now," he said. "It's going fast. That's the first thing Jim said when he saw me yesterday: 'I didn't think it was going to go this fast.'"

10

From the first, we'd known Jim to be nothing but active and strong. Winter and summer, in his ever-present billed cap and heavy black boots, he did all kinds of work from splitting firewood to fine carpentry to consulting on electrical problems for the school bus mechanic in town. He believed walking was bad for his heart, and explained that he didn't hunt or go into the woods anymore to make sure he wouldn't "overdo it," or "get carried away." But nothing in the way he lived suggested the two heart attacks serious enough for him to retire at fifty-eight. Just how long ago that was, we didn't learn for some time. Nor did he wear any mark of what he'd retired from: an engineering job at IBM.

He'd talk about it sometimes, his travels to exotic places, fine restaurants and fine wines, always emphasizing how well he had been treated, or how he'd amazed clients in Asia and Europe with his technical acumen. As he sat in our cabin, dressed in one of the faded long-sleeved flannel shirts he wore summer and winter, I tried to picture him in a dark suit, pressed shirt, necktie, boarding a plane, dining with foreign businessmen. It was a big stretch, all but unimaginable. Yet how likely was it that the man Jim appeared to be would care to pass much time with city folks like us?

With Bob, Jim discussed esoteric points of botany and other technical matters, from the mechanics and the aesthetics of photography to the workings of Ford engines. To me, he talked about gardening and cooking. He told me recipes as if they were stories, always leaving some secret ingredient or technique for the last, to build suspense. He was an adventurous eater, interested in new ideas and eager to try any weird thing I cooked up—something I appreciated, especially in an older person, since the elders I'd cooked for regularly (my parents and former in-laws) were militantly limited in their tastes, rarely crossing the boundaries of their personal culinary unknown, and then only with timidity and suspicion.

When he came to dinner, he always brought a bottle of wine, some vegetables from his garden, or a bag of Vermont apples. Occasionally I wondered why, with all his cooking talk, he'd only once brought something he'd prepared himself, an Easter bread. "Baked up a batch in Burlington," he said. The bread was good, but not what his hyperbole led one to expect. And most of the recipes he shared were simple, like green tomatoes—our neighborhood's primary crop—on the grill. To this day, whenever I eat beans fresh from the garden I think of Jim, and how he used to boast about putting away huge bowls of them, steamed just so in the microwave. "I make a whole meal out of 'em. And I tell you, that's some good eatin'." That was Jim's refrain, his slogan. Some good eatin'. You could almost hear him on a commercial.

It took me too long to catch on, but eventually, he told me he watched a lot of cooking shows on TV (thanks to the satellite dish that rose from the swamp behind his house) and, though he'd provide a blow-by-blow of the holiday feasts he and Duane and Duane's girlfriend, Carla, prepared together, I realized he hadn't even tried most of the cooking tips he passed along. I suspected some probably came from the local newspaper, which favored recipes featuring ingredients like miniature marshmallows or canned soup.

Where had I thought Jim acquired his culinary expertise? All on my own, I'd so romanticized his boyhood farm life in Vermont that I assumed it was the source of all he knew. Jim didn't talk at length about these years, and what little he did say suggested only that they were poverty-stricken and harsh. A five-mile walk to school on sub-zero mornings, in the dark. ("We didn't own a flashlight. Couldn't afford the batteries.") An overnight snowfall so deep he had to climb out an upstairs window to a shed roof and slide into a snowbank to get out to feed the animals. He'd left home at fourteen, he said, odd-jobbed his way to the Midwest, did a military stint, got some technical training and, in the early days of IBM, easily landed a job without an advanced degree.

Throughout the year, each time we came to the cabin, for two days or ten, we spent some of our precious time with Jim. I'd invite him for a meal, or he'd show up on his own and, like a kid come to play, participate in whatever we might be doing. We were essentially novices at country life, so ignorant about some things it's embarrassing to recall it. Jim loved this. It gave him an opportunity to shine, and he returned the favor with patience and generosity. He never laughed at our ignorance, and praise flowed from him as naturally as advice.

He'd admire our struggling garden, the first flowers and vegetables anyone had tried to wrest from this particular patch of rocky soil: the six-foot digitalis in their second bloom, monster tomato plants the summer I bagged fertilizer from an abandoned chicken coop. He tried with varying success to help Bob fix a succession of ailing cars. He'd attack any kind of problem with originality and verve, and some of his solutions were wonderfully practical. One warm day during our first winter, he found us in the woods trying to burn some brush in a little clearing. ("Thought I heard voices," he said.) A mere six inches of old snow lay on the ground, but we'd been trying to start our bonfire for nearly an hour and were about to give up.

"Well, you know, don't you, no matter how wet the woods are, doesn't matter, there's one place you can always find dry kindling?" We didn't. He smiled, the twinkle in his eye implying a fabulous surprise. After a pause sufficient to satisfy him that he'd raised the suspense a little, he strode over to a balsam tree, broke a few small dead twigs from the trunk, handed them to Bob, and we had a blaze going in no time.

This was a small favor, but there were huge ones, and because we could never get Jim to accept cash, even when he did something like coach Bob through a rewiring job that took nearly a week, we were constantly seeking ways to reciprocate. Clearly, he took pleasure in food, and after some trial and error we discovered what he liked best: fresh-baked bialys from New York City. Through the fall and spring and winter, we brought him a dozen each time we came up. And when I discovered the particular bialys he preferred above all others, I'd get up extra early to walk a mile each way to the shop that had them. The stock was limited; you had to get there before nine. Sometimes I had to twist my schedule into knots to work in those bialys. But this was the least we could do for Jim.

Not all of Jim's ideas were good ones. Some ran to the Rube Goldberg variety, and he'd spin them out as if white-knuckle drama were inherent in his plan to economize on electricity by rigging his wood furnace to double as a hot water heater. Further, he didn't hesitate to offer solutions to problems we *didn't* have, like delivering a twenty-minute monologue on how (and why) to grow potatoes in a stack of old tires. Some of his "solutions" made us recoil in horror. He hated the ubiquitous red squirrels, claimed they attacked his chipmunks, and took any opportunity to shoot the feisty rodents, usually from his kitchen window. And, after gunfire and a baseball bat had failed, he did away with garden-indulgent woodchucks by tossing a cocktail of clorox and ammonia down their hole and covering it with a rock.

Most troubling of all, though, was that Jim himself was a problem without any solution we ever found. It's an understatement to confess we weren't always glad to see him strolling down our path. The privacy for which we'd come here didn't include daily visits from a neighbor who liked to talk and talk and talk. He kept a polite distance when we had guests; otherwise, even when it was clear he was interrupting something, he seemed not to notice, and telling him seemed cruel. Clearly he was lonely. We didn't want to hurt his feelings. I remember standing on the lawn, shifting from one foot to the other, open paint-can in hand, while he delivered a monologue on how he'd stuffed the turkey he ate yesterday, and why the less enlightened never consider roasting a turkey in August, and why they should.

One afternoon when we were setting off to hike from a nearby trailhead, he passed in his car, stopped of course, and kept us for an hour, babbling that he was on his way to Vermont to buy his year's supply of paper plates, and how he calculated that using these paper plates was cheaper than running the hot water heater to wash dishes. Worst of all were unexpected visits when we were trying to pack up and leave at the end of a short weekend. Not only were we delayed in our return, but half the time, distracted, we'd leave important tasks undone or things forgotten.

When Jim dropped by when I was writing, Bob usually protected me by visiting with Jim outside and indicating I was busy. When Bob was in the mood, he also loved to tell and hear stories and I liked to tease him by saying he was a geezer-in-training under Jim and other elderly men with whom he'd while the time. In general, Bob dealt with Jim better than I did. In fact, despite all he did for us, for the first couple years I regarded the old man with some diffidence, almost as a necessary evil. His feelings toward me may have been similar: I think he was very fond of Bob, and tolerated me as part of the package, until our paths crossed one summer afternoon.

Jim was driving out to the main road; I'd gone for a walk in the same direction. When he stopped to say hello, I was kneeling alongside the road at the edge of our property, where I'd just discovered something in the sand.

"Whatcha got there?" he asked.

I broke off a few inches of wiry stem laden with tiny, ovate gray-green leaves.

"Taste this!"

He crushed the leaves between his fingers and sniffed. He smiled. Then he tasted, smiled again.

"Wild thyme?" I asked, though I knew.

"Sure is," he beamed. He got out of his truck and knelt beside me and together we studied the plant, the conditions in which it was growing, noted the big white pine that marked its location. He shook his head. "I didn't know about that," he said. I could tell he was impressed. I was pretty impressed myself. Thyme is a small plant, nothing showy, and this one wasn't even in flower. It looked like an easily transplanted thing, with rootlets coming all along the stem, and we each took a piece for our respective gardens.

For the rest of that summer and into the next, whenever Jim and I met, we'd report to each other like members of an investigative team.

"You know that street in town behind the laundromat? It's all over the sidewalk."

"Jerry Galusha's got it right through his pasture!"

We saw wild thyme along sandy roads, in abandoned fields off remote dirt tracks, between cracks in village sidewalks. At some folks' houses, it was an entire lawn, bursting at midsummer into a fragrant purple carpet. My transplant took and so did Jim's. And so, now, did our friendship.

Our favorite plants were those most people ignored or labeled weeds. We each spent a lot of time looking for them, moving them, nurturing them. Jim was always digging up something for me that he'd found on his land or in his travels; I returned the favor with a few herbs or flowers I'd managed to start on our city windowsills. The September when I learned of his illness, I was trying to acclimate to my inhospitable apartment a pot of fuchsia I'd nurtured from seedlings he'd given me in May.

At some point, I began giving Jim a kiss on the cheek when I hadn't seen him for a while, and before long we added a big hug. I recall the warmth in his eyes, his smile when he saw me, and it pleased me greatly that he could find something likeable in me—a person whose nature was so utterly different from his, someone of whom he could not possibly approve for the city ways she brought to the country—

someone who hurried, lacked patience, had deadlines, was often short of time. Regardless of whether I was glad to see him at a given moment, I'd come to love him as I love the best of my friends. When I realized he was ailing, I worried over him like family.

I'm not sure when he started feeling poorly. Jim was no complainer, but he hadn't seemed well in the spring—couldn't wait for warmer days. When summer came, he grumbled about the heat, said he couldn't sleep because his hip hurt. Arthritis, he said. It made sense to him that pain and lack of sleep should kill his appetite, but his loss of weight alarmed me, and I remember a steamy Sunday afternoon in July when I felt gratified to have got some cold watermelon soup into him. I wondered if he'd seen a doctor, but felt it was none of my business. Recalling his proud reports of "great" heart check-ups, I thought he probably had. Around mid-July, he said he had pills for the arthritis. From the side effects he described, I knew they were steroids. Surely the prescribing doctor was on top of things. Eventually, though, I learned that the pills, which had helped only briefly, had been prescribed for a friend who'd passed them on. By August, I was all but certain he was not getting help. Bob and I discussed how we might broach the subject with him, but got nowhere.

I thought about seeking the advice of some of the jolly, pink-cheeked elderly in the neighborhood. One day, I ran into a foursome at the post office, and the subject turned to Jim. I mentioned that he was complaining about not sleeping, and seemed to be having quite a bit of pain from his arthritis.

"Arthritis?" my friends hooted. "Tell us about it!"

I hadn't expected particular sympathy for Jim from these kind folks; I knew their scorn for his messy yard. But I hadn't realized this scorn extended to Jim himself. Or perhaps their dismissive response was directed not at Jim but at me, and they'd laughed at my ignorance of the fact that people of a certain age were never without aches and pains, and that Jim's problem was that he saw reason to complain of it. I didn't broach the subject again.

Had he been one of my city friends, I would have made sure he saw a doctor, even if I had to take him there myself. To press Jim on the subject, however, seemed presumptuous, almost insulting. Independence is a fierce thing in the mountains, especially in men of Jim's generation, a primary value maintained with an iron grip. Besides, the man had a wife. Surely she kept at least a minimal watch over his health, though he didn't seem to be getting over to Vermont every weekend anymore. First, Helen went to Florida to visit an old friend. Then there was a 4-H fair with the grandchildren. I began to wonder: was Helen some perverse invention? Had she been dead for years? True, she and Jim had allegedly taken a ten-day holiday together last fall, of which we'd heard all kinds of details, down to the mileage they put on the rental car. Still, we knew no one who had met her. Other than Jim's wedding ring, we had no empirical evidence of her existence, past or present.

In the last steamy days of August, Bob and I helped Jim put up his winter firewood. A neighbor on the main road had cut some good hardwoods to create a pond, and offered the wood to Jim. Jim's rusty brown truck was dead, and even though, in the way of older country men, he was as reluctant to accept help as he was eager to give it, he'd been talking all summer about borrowing our truck to get the firewood. Now, it was clear he didn't have the strength. So Bob sharpened up his chain saw and for several days running, picked up Jim in the morning and drove into the woods. From time to time I'd walk over to wherever they were working and help load or unload the truck. Jim was always glad to see me, but I could tell it made him uncomfortable to see a woman do this heavy work while he sat. As soon as I started to participate, he'd get up from his perch on a pile of logs and we'd have to persuade him to stay still.

We'd been back in the city less than two weeks when our upstream neighbor, Betty, phoned with the bad news. I called Jim at the hospital. He was as cheerful and optimistic as ever. He outlined the aggressive treatments, assured me he was not in pain, praised his doctors and the active role they'd established for him in his care. What he'd dismissed, at seventy-one, as arthritis had been diagnosed as cancer, widely metastasized, inoperable.

Hours later, I found myself in a Manhattan florist's, frustrated that I had no garden or meadow at hand, wishing I could at least choose from the great variety in the flower markets on upper Broadway to assemble the most beautiful bouquet he'd ever seen. I discussed the flowers to be wired him for an hour, as the florist phoned shops in Burlington to find out what they had. I was adamant that there be no chrysanthemums or other fall flowers. "A mixed spring bouquet?" the florist finally asked. We settled on lilies and snapdragons, a few roses, larkspur, delphinium.

Bob joined me and Duane on the path where we stood talking.

"Those were some beautiful flowers you sent," Duane said. Even yesterday, a week old, they were still going strong. And Jim loved them. "When they first came he couldn't stop talking about them." In the past few days, though, Jim was only intermittently alert. For the most part, medication was keeping him comfortable. But all treatment had been suspended.

Duane sighed deeply. "I got to ask you something. Did Jim ever say anything to you about having any children? Or did he ever mention another wife, before Helen?"

"No," I replied, surprised by the questions. "The only children he ever mentioned were Helen's. In fact, I thought there was only the daughter who lives with her, until he said something about a son winning some award."

"She has two sons. Two sons, and two daughters. But they're not Jim's. And he was married before her. Before his heart problems, he was married to someone else. He never said much about that. I asked him once, late one night when we were playing cards up at my place, if he had any kids, and he said, "Not that I know of."

"He never mentioned kids to me."

"I just wanted to make sure there wasn't someone I ought to get in touch with. The lawyer hasn't got there yet, and now it's the weekend. Jim asked me to look after things. He gave me his last wishes. There's no chance the lawyer'll be there until Monday, and that may be too late."

"Isn't Helen taking care of these things?"

Duane's brow pulled tight and his round face turned dark and angry. "I don't know what Helen's doing."

"She comes to the hospital, doesn't she?"

He shook his head. "Only once, far as I know, and that was when they admitted him. Supposedly she's coming today."

"Only once? Is she ill?" I recalled that when I'd asked Jim on the phone about Helen's visits he'd said she had a bad cold, and he didn't want her wearing herself out.

Duane went on. "I don't like to criticize or talk about what I don't know, and it's none of my business, but what the hell is she doing? The man is dying."

Tears filled his brown eyes and rolled down his cheeks. "Excuse me," he choked out. "I'm thirty years old. I never watched anybody die before. And he's my best friend," he told us. "He was like my father and my best friend at the same time."

Tears rose to my eyes, too. I reached out and put a hand on his arm, and we stood quietly for a moment.

"Have you actually seen Helen?" I asked.

"Yeah, I've seen her. I met her once years back. And I saw her just last week. Here. When she came to the house. I let her in. She was pretty pissed off. Not that I blame her. I was pretty shocked myself, when I went in there."

"You mean you hadn't been inside? Before that?"

"Nope. Never. You ever been in there?"

"No, but I was sure you…. And it was that bad?"

"You wouldn't believe how bad."

"When was the last time Helen saw it?"

"She said fourteen years."

We'd known Jim for some time before I took note that though he carried keys to our cabin, our car, and our beat-up red truck, we had never set foot beyond his door.

I'd considered this for the first time one fine August morning when I wanted his advice about putting up some jam, and couldn't figure out which door to knock on or where to leave a note. His current car was in the driveway, so it was a good bet he was home. But my repeated rapping at his front door brought no response, and the stoop was piled so high with newspapers, I decided he couldn't be using this egress. The basement/garage door was blocked by a small cement mixer. A back door hung, tight shut, some four feet from the ground with no stairs. I circled the house again, hoping I'd find him in the garden he talked about so much, but all I could find of the orderly, productive patch he'd proudly toured us through one summer was a row of six-pack seedlings half-hidden under a picnic table, more dead than alive. I finally left a note, along with the homemade blueberry muffins I'd brought, on the front seat of his car.

Of course we knew his house was a mess. We'd caught glimpses of things piled up, of general disorder. And his yard had become downright hazardous. He was on his third or fourth running vehicle since we'd met him, and the dead ones had accumulated, despite a lot of talk about plans to sell or part them off. Recent additions to what had once been the lawn were parts of the structure Duane had torn away in his renovation—large windows in heavy old wood frames, a small roof gable, slabs of siding. Every time I walked down his short driveway there'd be something new: a truck windshield, tubes of heating duct, a piece of culvert.

Jim had even joked about it. Once, he'd confided that Helen was thinking of retiring and leaving Vermont to live with him. He seemed to be looking forward to this. "But first I'll have to dehermitize," he'd said. "And that's gonna take a backhoe. If I can figure out how to get a backhoe in the house."

Still, it had never occurred to me that he invited no one—not even Duane—inside.

By the time Jim's firewood was all cut and stacked, our summer was over. Busy packing to return to Manhattan and trying to finish all the season's last chores, we expected Jim to just turn up, as he always did when we were leaving. I'd catch myself listening for the rumble of his car on the bridge, but the silence of the road was unbroken. He could die in there all alone, I thought, and no one would know.

Early on a lovely Sunday afternoon, the time came to leave.

Bob phoned Jim, and to our relief, he quickly answered. But no, he didn't feel well enough to come out today. He'd just been napping. I wanted to return a cookbook he'd loaned me. Could I bring it by? Did he want me leave it in his car? No need, he said. Just leave it on our kitchen table and he'd pick it up.

I picture the quiet road in the gentle shade of a September morning. The warblers and the hummingbirds, the phoebes and the kingfishers have all flown; only the ravens crack the silence as they patrol the stream. It's not a Friday, Jim's regular Burlington day. Nonetheless, he's preparing to carry out the decision made during the last of a string of sleepless nights: to drive to Burlington and see a doctor. He'd like to wait until Friday—it makes him queasy to do something so out of form—but he's growing weaker every day.

He double-checks the timer that will light his window at dusk, leaves a house key under a cinderblock to which he'll direct Duane. Feeds some peanuts to his chipmunks. Drives the few hundred yards to our place, unlocks our door and picks up his cookbook. In its place on the dark oak table, he leaves a note: He's going to Burlington to stay until he's better, he writes, and, as an afterthought, scrawls a phone number—Helen's—underneath. And despite a sinking feeling in his heart, and his insides and his old bones racked with pain, he drives out on the old farm road, thinking he feels just a little stronger already.

Two hours later, he pulls into the hospital parking lot and goes straight to emergency. When they tell him he'll have to stay, he phones Duane in New Jersey.

"He told me where the key was, and said, 'You go in there,'" Duane told us. "'There's valuables in that house.' And he told me where the firearms were, and said to take them out and hang on to them for him."

A few days later, as soon as he arrived, Duane did just this (at least so I believe) and to the extent that he could, tried not to see what he couldn't help seeing until Helen came the next week and they went in together.

The hospital bed was cranked to a sitting position. There was an IV, but no elaborate rigs or tubes. Too weak to lift his head from the pillow, Jim raised his arm, with great effort, to extend his hand, which I pressed in both of mine as I kissed his cheek. His cheek was hot, his hand cold, but his grip powerful as ever. He was cheerful and glad to see us. His eyes were clear and sharp. Not in much pain, he said. But it was difficult for him to talk. He introduced us to the pleasant elderly couple who were settled in the visitors' chairs. But I didn't quite understand who they were. Sociable Bob did his best to make conversation, but I could tell Bob had no idea who they were, either. Where was Helen?

The flowers I'd wired were on their last. I tossed the wilted bouquet, got fresh water, arranged the snapdragons I'd brought.

The gentleman offered me his chair and as I sat and faced Jim, I took in his altered appearance and puzzled over exactly what was so different. The rest of his body wasted, his hands looked larger than ever, the wide gold wedding band still snugly in place. Of course it was strange seeing him in bed, seeing his chest, scrawny and white through the folds of the hospital gown, but far stranger, I realized, was seeing him hatless without actually seeing him remove his hat, to hold it in his hand, place it beside him on the table, hang it on the hook by our door. There was no hat in sight. Not only had he almost no hair, but almost no eyebrows; I hadn't noticed this before.

And something else was missing. Something I found it hard to get a fix on. After a time, I realized it was only that Jim always wore something black, which looks odd on an old man in the mountains, where only bikers wear it. He had rugged but incongruously elegant slip-on boots he'd found on sale in one of Lake George's upscale outlets—not the rough brown work boots everyone else wore. And sometimes he wore a short black leather jacket, as deeply cracked and creased with age as his own face.

And of course, at the last, this man who loved so much to talk was doing no talking.

Wasn't he cold? The blanket was so thin, the hospital gown half-open. Did he want another blanket? No, he was fine.

I thought of the deep sub-zero days and nights when he'd come to while away some time at our cabin, dressed in layers of clothes, but skimpily, clothes that never looked warm enough to me, that didn't seem like half as much as I was wearing.

There were a few cards on the nightstand, but no, no one else from the neighborhood—except for Duane, of course—had visited, he said. I don't know who I expected would have made the four-hour round trip. But he had so many cronies, didn't he? People he talked about all the time, most of whom I didn't know. And what about Helen? Oh, she'd be by later, couldn't say when.

Duane soon appeared. He'd just gone for some lunch, he said.

And then, there was nothing to say, though we all probably could have stood on the road and chatted for hours. Indoors, anywhere indoors, it would be different. But here Bob and I were in a hospital room with Duane, who'd heard our mutual friend's last wishes, who'd been by his side almost constantly for the last few days. It must please Jim at least a little, I thought, to see his silently warring neighbors not merely civil, but smiling warmly to each other at last. I imagined he had some homily for the equation that had brought us together, or that he was congratulating himself on the correctness of his belief that we would come to appreciate each other one day.

While the elderly pair said their goodbyes to Jim, Bob and I went out to confer with Duane in the visitors' lounge.

He explained that something about the location of the tumor in Jim's neck or brain was, mercifully, blocking much of the pain he otherwise would be experiencing.

We told Duane we'd be here a while, if he wanted to go home, but he said he wasn't planning to go home tonight.

"I'm staying the night. I'm not leaving him here alone. I've been trying to find someone who can tell me if there's a place in the building where I can shower and change my clothes, is all. Then I'll be fine."

Duane made much of the fact that Jim didn't have a will, wanted to make one. There had been some complication about Helen's getting a lawyer to the hospital, though Jim had requested it several days ago. Tomorrow might be too late, Duane repeated.

Money? No, Jim never had more than what was in his pocket. Yes, there had been an IBM pension, but he'd retired so early, it wasn't what it might have been. It didn't go that far. There were property taxes on two places. A mortgage on the house here in Vermont.

As for Helen, "Don't get me started," Duane said, shaking his head.

When we came back into the room, a pleasant-looking gray-haired woman was sitting at the bedside, holding Jim's hand, and helping him drink some water. Fussing over him and calling him "Sweetie." Helen, at last! No. It was his sister, come from Boston. Jim was her baby brother, and she frankly adored him.

When we left, well after nightfall, I kissed his hot forehead. I can still feel the indomitable strength with which he squeezed my hand. I couldn't bring myself to say goodbye.

They'd threaded their way into the house on a narrow path, Duane and Helen and some of her children, on the day Duane turned over to Helen the key to her husband's domain. The path, a sort of canyon, actually, wound from the door through the kitchen and down a hall to the end of a back room where a La-Z-Boy recliner faced the TV. Apart from the recliner, in which Jim had told me he'd slept most of the summer, every surface, including the bed, was covered with debris piled several feet deep. On either side of the path, and throughout the rest of the house were walls of trash. The top layer was composed primarily of copies of the Glens Falls *Post Star* (descending chronologically to a date some fifteen years back, they would discover weeks later, when they finally struck bottom). Sandwiched between the layers of newspaper and plastered to these papers with various kinds of incrudescence were the famous paper plates, heaped with chicken bones and other less identifiable remains of meals, and bags and bags of untouched groceries: meat rotted in its cellophane, store-bought vegetables encased in gray-green fur, the tiny skeletons of red squirrels—yes, the rodents I'd heard him shooting from his house had been *inside* the house—left to decompose where his bullets had felled them. Woven throughout were trails of used toilet paper.

They flung the doors and windows wide, then ran outside, choking for air. Someone went to the supermarket and bought all the kitty litter in stock. With it, they thickly covered the exposed flooring and other naked surfaces. They returned two weeks later, the day after the funeral. The stench had dissipated into the oncoming winter and the excavation could begin.

11

All this Bob and I began to piece together on a raw November day. It was our first weekend at the cabin since Jim's death. In Duane's virginal model-house kitchen, we spoke sadly about Jim, and Duane, pale and subdued, told us that Jim's last wishes had been for Helen to take things slow, not to get all worked up and act too quickly. She had a tendency to want to do everything all at once, Jim had said. He wanted her to think things through. He didn't want her to wear herself out. But, with the help of her four children and their spouses and some dozen grandchildren, she'd been doing exactly what Jim had hoped she wouldn't: rapidly emptying the house, giving away valuables to strangers, paying people to cart off stuff she could have sold. Duane had brought several large items, like the cement mixer, over to his place "So they wouldn't just disappear," he said. "She can get money for that stuff. And it's not like she doesn't need it. She's not going have an easy time selling that house. The basement's filled with water half the year. The roof's shot. I'm not sure about the well. I thought my friend Jack might try to buy it—you know Jack, from the white house up by town—but the place is too far gone even for him."

Bob and I looked at each other. It was with this Jack that Duane had shared his rowdiest entertainments. If he did buy Jim's house, we'd move.

Yes, Helen would definitely be there today. She'd been coming with her children every weekend—just the daughters, now, the sons had gone back out west. "I'm trying to help her, like I promised Jim I would. But she doesn't make it easy."

From the window, we saw that two station wagons had pulled up across the road. Three heavy-set women and assorted children were milling about Jim's driveway.

"They're here," Duane said. "Let's go."

She was a tall woman in her sixties, with curly light brown hair and a pretty face. Her eyes were strikingly blue, like Jim's, but even kinder than his, darker in color and softer in mood. Her look was gentle, complicated, bewildered. And she was flanked by two fiery, articulate daughters poised to put their substantial bodies in harm's way to protect her. But Helen seemed more than capable of taking care of herself.

Before Bob and I could introduce ourselves, she opened with a volley of accusations at Duane: *What had happened to the cars?*

I both felt and saw Duane's shock at the assault—as if a physical blow had sent him reeling backwards. "You said you wanted them out of here by this weekend," he replied. "I was trying to do what you asked...."

The daughters, acerbic with fury, bristling with intelligence, picked up the attack, and Duane didn't have a prayer.

It was all coming too quick and angry for us to follow the story straight through, but it seemed to go something like this:

As the family took on the task of emptying Jim's house, they'd used the dead cars to assemble and temporarily store some things they'd eventually take home.

"There were things in those cars that we needed."

"Important papers."

"Things we wanted."

The vehicles themselves—particularly the rusty brown truck with the snowplow—were to go to Jim's pal, Jerry, at the garage in town.

"Jerry couldn't take them until next week," Duane tried to explain. "You wanted them out...I was just trying to do what you asked...."

It was difficult to resist the impulse to intercede. Surely these savvy women knew that even in the mountains it's not a simple matter to dispose of four senescent, unlicensed, unstartable vehicles at a moment's notice. But the women wouldn't let him get a sentence out intact, and Duane almost immediately abandoned all defense and descended—a sheer drop—into passivity. I recognized the posture—an edge of stoicism in the slump of defeat—of a man who simply refuses to do battle with strong or emotional women. In men close to me, it had made me furious. In Duane, I found it more than sad, almost sordid. I want to shake him, tell him to stand up for himself. And how all this conflict and vituperation would have distressed Jim!

As the four small children scampered down to the stream to play, the six adults—each of us sipping from the rapidly chilling cups of coffee with which we'd arrived—sat on the unpainted wood steps, on rocks or stumps, on an upturned plastic milk crate. Except for a few feeble interjections, Bob and I kept a stunned silence as the fur flew, until Duane, a whipped dog, simply slunk back across the road.

"I don't think he meant any harm," I finally ventured. "There must have been some misunderstanding. He was devoted to Jim. I can't believe he'd deliberately go against your wishes."

Even as I spoke, I had to ask myself why I was doing this: Before Helen and her formidable daughters, I found myself defending the man I'd have less than two months ago gladly run out of the neighborhood. I could feel how alone he felt, how bereft, how he wanted to do the right thing, even if he wasn't sure how. And I didn't believe in the venality Helen attributed to him.

But why should they care what I believed?

Even with all Duane's disturbing comments about Helen's behavior while Jim was in the hospital, we'd been prepared to meet a family in mourning, and to offer condolences and help. Clearly, neither was wanted. Perhaps the use of our truck? Not met with the enthusiasm I'd naively expected, we were nonetheless not turned away.

Someone pointed to the lawnmower and cement mixer on Duane's porch, implying he'd stolen them. I found no reason to doubt he'd taken these things for safekeeping, as he'd told us. But it would be no surprise if he lacked the common sense to carry out good intentions in an appropriate way.

I tried to explain our closeness to Jim, and to make it clear that, even though we were speaking in Duane's defense, we weren't to be lumped with him.

"He worshipped Jim. He wants to do the right thing. He's very young. We don't know him all that well, and frankly, it wouldn't surprise me if he did something stupid. But a thief? I'd find that hard to believe."

It took longer than perhaps it should have for me to realize that every time we said, or even implied, something positive about Jim the less these people wanted to do with us. And the less inclined I was to simply leave. I felt that we represented Jim today, the Jim we knew, and that someone should stand, at least in these few hours, for the consummate good neighbor who had spent the last decade of his life alone on this road, and who had become so quickly obscured by what he'd left behind. And despite their wariness, the women kept talking to us, though the emotions were so charged, so vengeful, the content so unexpected, I could only partly follow what they said.

They'd had the electricity turned off, so they had only the short hours of daylight in which to accomplish tasks they described as "overwhelming" and "disgusting." (They frequently applied this last adjective to Jim, too.) This was all taking too long and costing too much. They couldn't put the house on the market before they cleaned it out, and if they didn't finish before it got too cold or a big snow fell, either of which could happen anytime, it would have to wait until spring, and they had to have the house sold by then.

They talked about all that had to be carted off, about an outbuilding scheduled to be torn down by someone who'd been promised scrap metal in payment. Now the scrap metal had turned up gone! Posted signs and padlocks had gone up right away, but theft had begun almost as quickly. Was this why they were so wary of us? We finally convinced them we didn't want anything, and they accepted our offer to load our truck with the stacks of newspapers they were heaving out onto the stoop, and haul them to the dump.

We could have just turned away and gone home. But there *was* something we wanted: answers, clues even, to a jumble of questions just beginning to form. We were just a few hundred yards from our house, but what *was* this place? We were disoriented, hoping for something in the revelations that kept tumbling one upon the other, that would help us construct some sort of roadmap to this new terrain. It was utterly preposterous that all this had been right here without our knowing it. And yet, I still believed in the Jim I'd known. I wanted to do one last thing for him, and I knew exactly what he would have wanted: for me to assist Helen.

I couldn't help but like her. Even her outrage expressed more shock than bitterness. As soon as I caught her in a quiet moment, I asked, "How long since you were here?" We were standing at the bottom of the driveway. We both looked up toward the house.

"Well, just a year ago, last fall, when we came back from our trip." As Helen went on, it was obvious, to my relief, that all Jim had told us about the trip was true. They'd traveled south in a car rented in Burlington, and in which Helen had picked him up here and dropped him off. "But I left him right here, on the road, right where we're standing. I didn't even go up the driveway. I didn't go inside. I wanted to. He wouldn't let me. 'Couldn't I just come in for a minute?' I asked him. 'I want to see what the old place looks like.' 'No, you don't want to,' he told me. 'Not now.' I should have insisted, I suppose.... But I never imagined anything like this. When we came to turn off the water, after he was in the hospital, I didn't know what to expect. But I never could have imagined this. If he hadn't died I'd've killed him."

Her gentle eyes belied her words. It was impossible, I sensed, for this woman to bear malice to anyone—even her maddening late husband. For her daughters, however, it was different. The younger women perceived Jim's very existence as an affront, as if his life had had a single purpose, manifested in this house: to commit a grand act of hostility to their mother and to them.

"He was like this all his life. He trashed our lives before, and now —this."

"He stole our childhood."

"For fourteen years, he didn't throw a single thing away."

"You know about the pit out back?"

We didn't. They led us past the vegetable garden, its fence of chicken wire tacked to cedar posts still tight and neat, into a narrow, pretty strip of young white pines, beyond which lay the swamp and the satellite dish. And there, no more than a hundred yards from the road, but obscured by the pines until you were right upon it, was a huge hole. He'd had it dug, I supposed, when the backhoe came to scoop out Duane's new basement. Twisted metal and wire stuck up from its depths. Cans—not from foodstuffs, but from chemicals—littered its banks. He'd dumped his sludgy motor oil here when he changed it, old antifreeze, containers from chain saw fuel, who knew what.

"This is what your good neighbor did with his backyard," said one of the daughters.

"His toxic waste dump," the other sneered. "His Superfund site."

"You hated him," I said, and immediately felt foolish.

"He hated us."

"He never even called us by our names."

Jim, who'd never had an unkind word to say about anyone?

The young woman jerked her head toward the dilapidated house. "This was our inheritance. This was our college tuition. This was our mother's retirement."

I thought of the beautifully kept homes—modest but tasteful, with riotous gardens—of retired couples I knew here, who gave their thirty-acre kingdoms storybook names like "Frogmore" and "Hummingbird Hollow." Perhaps such a place was what Helen had expected for her retirement. And why not?

"He spoke of your mother as if she were a saint," I said.

"Mother *is* a saint," snapped the daughter.

I felt slapped. But I understood their rage. It echoed the rage that had intermittently stabbed at the center of our lives for six years as, one by one, the elders of Bob's family—father, mother, aunt—passed on, leaving him and his sister to grasp the loose ends of three sudden deaths, dismantle two households, tidy the messes of disordered decades. Bob became depressed. His sister responded with a seething anger that became the focus for all the disappointments of her life; for her, the chaos left by the aunt in the dementia of her old age became the full measure of the woman's years.

Trying to convey to Helen's daughters that I recognized their fury as coming from great hurt, and didn't condemn it, I began talking about our experiences cleaning out Bob's parents' large house, and his aunt's squalid apartment. Something in my stories turned the women around. There was a moment when they suddenly looked at me as if seeing me for the first time, and decided I was all right.

"Have you been inside? We took pictures because no one would believe us. It's already two hundred percent better than it was. You haven't seen it? Come."

And so I finally stepped into Jim's inner sanctum.

This was no hermit's cabin. It was a two-story house with a full basement, designed for a family of six. A narrow central hallway bisected the first floor, front door to back, and off this hall were half a dozen rooms of indeterminate purpose. At every random place where my eyes managed to focus on something beyond the detritus, what I saw was incomplete, nonfunctional, destroyed. A stove top that had never been connected, a hearth without firebrick. The images blurred. It was more than the eye could take in. You couldn't see the walls. It was hard to pick out any detail from the piles and heaps.

I understood at once why Helen had been storing things in cars. Inside, no surface was clean enough to serve as a base for establishing order. It was hard to imagine even looking for such things as "documents." But if you were to happen on something of value, the first impulse of any sane person would be to walk it out the door.

As they told us about putting down the kitty litter, and began to describe what they'd found on their first foray inside, my head reeled. How could it be that we hadn't known the person about whom this house made testament? Had we made too little of the condition of his yard? My mind turned again and again to the carpentry job our good neighbor Jim had once done to mouseproof our kitchen cabinets in our absence. It was not only perfectly executed, but so neat I couldn't tell he'd been in the house until I opened the cabinets and saw that the job was complete. He'd left not even a speck of sawdust.

The daughters had said Jim didn't wash and that the tub had never been used. I didn't believe this. But I saw with my own eyes that the part about the tub was true: on its blue vinyl surface, under a gray film, were large paper labels, nearly a foot square, that no drop of water had touched.

"When I was a little girl, I asked my mother if Jim showered at work, because I knew he never took a bath at home," said one daughter.

"When Mother went on that trip and had to ride in the car with him, she kept the windows open all the time," said the other.

I was dumfounded. Jim had never seemed dirty to us, all those times he'd sat at our dinner table, in the closed-up winter cabin, in scrappy layers of clothes that never seemed to me to add up to enough warmth. We knew he didn't swim. "Never learned how," he'd said. I wondered if he hadn't bathed at Duane's. He'd once mentioned going "to the grocery store across the street"—meaning Duane's kitchen—for a can of mushrooms. Why not use Duane's sauna or Jacuzzi as well? But why not use his own tub? This he clearly had not done. The bathroom sink with its fading paper labels, was equally virginal. In the kitchen, a double basin of stainless steel was blackened to a bubbly char, apparently caused by the darkroom chemicals heaped on the counter next to an old photo enlarger. There was no functional stove or refrigerator in the kitchen, either. A microwave and a hot plate sat on the basement's dirt floor. ("It's a wonder he never electrocuted himself or burned the place down," Helen marveled.) Also in the basement were several refrigerators and freezers, unplugged and brimming with food.

But the most significant thing about the house was what they did not find amid the garbage and the stench: what they did not find was bugs. The rotten meat should have been crawling with maggots, the spilled sugar with ants, the dusty eaves with spiders. But there was not a single insect. We knew Jim always kept the windows closed. We hadn't known until Duane told us, that Jim had periodically fogged the place with pesticide bombs, and never bothered to leave or even air the place out. Helen's daughters theorized that these toxins were the source of Jim's cancer, so generalized through bones, brain, stomach, liver, virtually every part of his body, that its primary site had not been identified.

"There he was all alone in that house," Bob mused that evening. "There was no one to challenge the way he lived. He could do anything he wanted—including creating his own silent spring."

All through that weekend and other weekends that fall, the story came to us—in a rush, it seemed, and yet in bits and shards.

I kept expecting Duane to show up with the contents of the cars, to say he'd undone whatever he wasn't supposed to have done with them, but Duane stayed in his house.

Snow came late that year, hard frost still later. We visited our cabin every two or three weeks, and each time there were more tools and gadgets and mounds of wet sheetrock in Jim's yard. From the basement came hunks of steel and iron, parts of some huge machine or many machines unidentifiable to us, along with roomsful of brand new ruined furniture, delivered more than a decade ago, never unpacked, the staples in the water-logged cartons intact.

I began to understand that Jim's house was a dream interrupted, frozen at some moment fourteen or more years ago, whenever someone had hammered a last nail, halting the construction midstream. It existed in two time zones simultaneously, one represented by the rotted cartons of new furniture, the other by the accumulations of the years and entropy's unchallenged march.

Word quickly got around that the house was being emptied. Helen blamed this on Duane. He'd told people Jim was in the hospital, though she'd asked him not to, and even, we heard in town, went about asking for contributions for him—a solicitation not well-received in a community that wouldn't forgive a man for keeping out-of-state plates on his car. But others might have spread the word as well: Hunting season had begun, always the busiest time on the road, and this year, the loggers engaged by Ernie Martin came through often as well, and saw Jim's yard filling up with piles of things. Even on the day we first met Helen, when the yard was relatively empty, as we moved in and out hauling trash, some part of my distracted mind registered that there were quite a number of vehicles going up the road. Hunters, I thought at first. Then I realized the same pick-ups and vans that seemed to be heading for deeper woods were too soon coming back down. Jim's place was being cruised.

As the contents of the house flowed out, Dickensian characters who looked as if they lived in coal mines crawled from their crumbling trucks whenever the place was unattended by Helen's family, and scavenged at will. When we strolled by to check things out, they claimed to be Jim's friends, squinted at us with toothless grins and sent the little children they always brought—their grandbabies, they called them—off to play among barrels of nameless chemicals and heaps of scrap metal and broken glass.

And on and on, the revelations, like Jim's things, tumbled forth: That it was the junk that had ended his marriage to Helen. "He was filling our house with it," one of her daughters explained. "There was no room for us or our things. She asked him for a divorce. He cried and begged and threatened to kill himself. Finally she told him to go and live here and she wouldn't divorce him as long as he left us alone. And that's what he did."

That not only had he spent on this house all the money left to Helen's children by their natural father, but that he'd built it with their unwilling labor.

That everything he owned, like the refrigerators and the freezers, he owned in multiples: dozens of hammers and measuring tapes, hundreds of keys. (Helen wanted to return these to their owners but finally had to admit it was hopeless to try to identify all the houses they unlocked.) There were redundancies of tinned food in cases. Bottles of olive oil and cartons of bagged popcorn, paper plates and cups sealed in their packaging, enough to party the entire town twice over. Even his strange cap with the cartoon dinosaurs had a hundred mates, brand new in a carton. ("One of his get-rich schemes," sneered a daughter.) He was poorer, it turned out, than we had imagined, for everything he didn't spend "stocking up," he invested in "schemes" that lost every dime.

And his name wasn't Jim at all. It was Willard.

In the mountains, one frequently hears stories of people who go out walking, get lost, and are never found, or found too late.

In the 1950s there was a middle-aged man, well-known around the hiking lodges of the High Peaks, who came to the Adirondacks for a few weeks each summer. He hiked each day, always alone, and always returned in time for dinner. One morning, he set off to climb Boreas Mountain and was never seen again. Investigators discovered he'd used several different names, each with its separate identity, in the various inns he'd frequented. In one he was known as a salesman, in another a medical doctor, at a third, some sort of writer. No kin could be found; no one ever learned who he actually was. Perhaps someone will yet find his bones on the broad summit of Boreas, where the krummholz of stunted spruce and balsam grows so dense that a small wrecked airplane lay there for two decades before a hiker happened upon it and its skeletal pilot.

Sometimes hikers who go missing in summer are found in fall. Strayed from a marked trail, they fall afoul of tangled backcountry, eluding search parties among ferns and foliage too dense to easily sustain human passage. In autumn, as summer's dark woods open up, ways through unmarked country show plain; hunters know them well.

A few years before we bought the cabin, Bob and I drove up from Manhattan for a July Fourth camping trip, only to find ourselves in the middle of a manhunt for a backpacker who'd vanished in mid-June. He'd set out alone on a popular trail, where he'd signed in at all the designated checkpoints—until, some 50 miles into a 132-mile trip, his tracks went cold. The night we arrived, dogs and helicopters were on their way from far and wide. As we set up our tent in the dark, I pictured the poor man at my shoulder, trapped behind the forest's curtain. Whatever had happened to him, it could as easily have happened to us. Back in Manhattan, all through that summer, I thought often of this man, about whom I knew almost nothing. Every few weeks I rode the subway to a midtown library to scan the Albany papers for an update on the search. By the end of July, more than two hundred volunteers had combed the woods without finding a clue. In mid-August I learned that, clueless still, they'd given up.

On the first day of rifle season, deer hunters came upon his final campsite; his body was found nearby, face down in a shallow stream. It was early October. Autopsy showed he'd lived through August before succumbing to exposure, was alive all those weeks I and so many others had been thinking about him. His campsite was a scant three miles from a large public campground and a well-traveled road. In his journal he'd noted tying a red T-shirt to a tree, keeping his campfire going all night, and screaming at the helicopters he saw overhead. Hard as they'd tried, the searchers had been unable to see the lone man they were looking for, lost among summer's lush distractions. In the woods, what summer hides, autumn tells.

And so it was with Jim in his last summer, desperate for a lifeline, the truths of his whereabouts as hidden from himself as from anyone, to become plain as bare earth in November. Exiled to the mountains, cut off, ambivalent perhaps about whether he wanted to be rescued or found out, he prowled the dark scary forest of his house, turning and returning to the tattered La-Z-Boy recliner as his only landmark. Sidetracked every day in a million tiny ways, he was captive of his compulsions, unable to bring the simplest acts to completion. How many times had he set out to pot up his six-pack seedlings, or make Helen a hanging basket, and hit a wall of darkness, a tangle of alder, and been forced to turn back and try another way? I know this dead end like the taste of the endless cups of coffee I pour to move myself along through certain fruitless days. I could picture in anyone the seed of all Jim was, and could easily imagine myself if not on this same dark path, on some other, equally compelling and futile.

I'm not sure if I found it more frightening that, losing the neighbor I'd known, I'd discovered a stranger had sat at my table—or that I knew this stranger, too. As soon as we returned to the city after our first encounter with Helen, Bob and I started throwing things away. The clutter in our booklined apartment had become foreboding, a symptom. And in the dark days of the late fall and winter, as I sat alone there with my work, my mind often turned to Jim's solitary life. My world was shaken. If so much of Jim could be so invisible to us, who was less mysterious? Wasn't it arrogant to think it "impossible" that all this could be next door without our knowing? How different were Jim's secrets from the passions of an adulterous heart beating against the breast of an unsuspecting mate? Were they different from the dreaming mysteries of any lover asleep on the pillow beside us? Or of the child or parent whose soft, even breath lulls us from the adjacent room?

As the year grew cold, I wondered what Jim had thought about, alone in his almost windowless house on such blustery days, and why he'd clung to everything he got his hands on. Even his "toxic waste dump" was in essence not a place for discarding things but for saving them.

In his chaos, I saw torment; there lay the loneliness that not a single soul had recognized. No one saw past the neighborliness, generosity and strong helping hands, through the layers of boastfulness and braggadocio and false self-sufficiency to the neediness that made him save his chicken bones.

Helen had been his sole anchor point. Coming and going from his world like fair weather, Bob and I and Duane were merely the flimsiest of handgrips in a long precipitous fall. But even his love for Helen hadn't kept the abyss at bay. Not when they lived together nor in the fourteen years of Fridays when he had gone to Burlington to court her. Each Friday that last spring, they'd lunched—if he'd told me once, he'd told me twenty times—on the long-stemmed California strawberries he'd brought from some Glens Falls supermarket, served with powdered sugar and Grand Marnier. When he'd gleamed and glowed at us over her enjoyment of the strawberries, he was assuring himself that the courtship was going well; he'd win back his Helen's hand. If Jim's house was "her retirement," as Helen's daughters said, she must have given him some future to cling to. All he had to do was to "dehermitize" as he put it. But he couldn't do that to save his soul. I'd never thought of busy, affable Jim as a hermit. But of course, by exile if not by choice, that's what he was.

Jim's house was empty and boarded up before the first snow blanketed the yard, leaving it, for any passerby who didn't know what lay beneath, as tidy as an empty table.

At Christmas time, gathering boughs for the mantel, I went behind

Jim's house and cut a few branches of white pine. I looked for Jim, but he wasn't there.

In January, the Martins' logging shifted my focus from Jim. But I was still haunted by the way he'd smiled as he strolled into our garden, by how pleased I'd been when he'd admired the progress of my flowers. It was hard to explain to my city friends why I was taking Jim's death so hard. But I was having trouble getting through my days. Remorse and self-blame swelled my loss. Couldn't I have saved him somehow? Doubt was my constant companion. Part of what I'd lost was the certainty that he had been my friend. Maybe he hadn't even liked me. Then this thought stabbed with a twist: I'd taken his affection as the acceptance of the land itself, read in his smile words like "City girl, you're okay." His stepdaughters had called him a manip- ulator, a charmer. "He fooled you," they'd all but told me. Had he? Was it manipulation, or was it my seeing only what I could recognize and label that made me feel he accepted me exactly as I was? As I was? Nonsense. He knew some of my surfaces, some of what I cared about. Had he known *me* any better than I'd known him? He had no idea who, in sum, I was. Yet, what he saw, I thought, was something essen- tial. And it had seemed enough.

Gazing out the cabin window on a February afternoon, I watched the snow slowly blanketing our small, vast world. Daydreaming into the silent rhythm of the white veil as it fell, I remembered the August day we unloaded the last of Jim's firewood in his driveway, and how disturbed I'd felt when I noticed a flat of freesias, half covered by the corner of a blue tarp, still struggling to live after a summer of neglect. The day he'd bought them, he'd presented two to me as a special gift. In spite of it all, he was my friend, the old man of the forest, whose life, in a separateness and privacy I'd chosen to respect, had disinte- grated virtually under my eyes. The one thing I wished I'd known sooner was that Jim wasn't anyone's. And if I had known? I couldn't have protected him from the wild thicket of his nature anymore than I could save the Martins' land from being logged.

Up the road the logging went on, but I didn't go there anymore, couldn't bear to see. When I crossed the bridge that winter, I went only as far as Jim's house, to see if the For Sale sign was still there. Until the fate of that house was settled, our future on the road remained uncertain. We wanted to add on to our cabin, and to put up a small studio back in the woods, but we would do nothing until we knew who our new neighbors would be. Having assured myself the sign still stood, I had no reason to linger, but I did. I stood in the icy driveway, and stared at the silent house, so familiar, so strange. I stood there until my fingers numbed in my mittens and my eyes stung from the cold. I was still looking for some way in.

By March a pending sale was rumored, and before the snow melted, the sign had been removed. We didn't know the couple who bought the place, but we might have: Ralph, a big, booming man about my age, was an engineer at the same huge bank where my brother was an officer. When they were introduced on our lawn, they recognized each other from the elevators and corridors of a skyscraper 250 miles south. Ralph had a biting wit that was nicely balanced by the softer humor of his petite wife, Angie, who always had a perfect manicure, even when stripping furniture. Though this was the third house the couple had set out to rescue from the brink of ruin, they were unprepared for the four feet of water that inundated the basement with the spring thaw, for the red squirrels that persisted in invading through the attic, and for many other consequences of Jim's bizarre decisions. And they were unprepared for Duane. Like us, they'd bought a place that faced a pristine forest. By the time they moved in, their front door looked out on the silver shine of the insulation that was the exterior of Duane's house.

Immediately after Jim's death, Duane had stayed alone on the road for most of the fall, and then stayed away. Over the winter, we heard rumors: that he'd lost his job, that he was ill, that his girlfriend, Carla, was ill, that he'd had a nervous breakdown, that his finances were in ruin.

I have no idea if any of this was true. But I know that in that lonely hunting season when Mr. R. began the logging of Ernie Martin's land, Duane's grief was compounded by the rage of Helen's injustice. He'd kept a deathbed vigil in her stead; he'd heard his friend's last wishes—"Help Helen"—and tried to fulfill them, only to be called a liar and a thief. Alone except for the logging trucks that rumbled past his door each day, he stepped out to the road one frosty morning, stopped Mr. R. and made a deal for the cutting of his trees. Or maybe Mr. R. stopped him. Either way, in a manner his beloved Jim never would have permitted, Duane denuded the stream that linked us all, and left a scene as ravaged as if he'd ripped every living thing out of the earth with his own hands.

PART V

Disturbed Ground

*Ironically, the cycles of heavy use that have
periodically threatened the northeastern forests
have been partially caused or at least made
possible by the forest's remarkable resilience.
Even in the face of rough treatment, these woods
have wanted to grow back and they usually
do…some have cited this resilience to justify
heavy cutting; others…fear that heavy use will
destroy the complexity that makes the forest so
resilient in the first place.*

Contested Terrain, Philip G. Terrie

*…in the North Woods a long time ago
Certain trees were folks; people went to see them
As great persons in the neighborhood. It seemed
They gave counsel with leaves and needles
And bark that the mountain folk understood.*

The Old Pine Tree, Jeanne Robert Foster

12

Five years have passed since the night we lost our way in the beech grove. The spot where we saw the last red blaze among enchanting trees can't be much more than two or three miles from our cabin. We have never tried to find it again. Should we look this afternoon? Probably not. I never asked Herman whether those beech trees belonged to his family or to another private owner, or to the State of New York. If those great trees among the mysterious cairns grew on state land, they are probably there still, even more magnificent in their gentle austerity than they were five years ago. If they were the Martins' trees, they're gone. Either way, I won't see the beech grove again. I forego certainty of its fate in deference to the remembered magic of its beauty in the long midsummer twilight.

We do, however, walk up to the farm in search of ripe apples.

Most of the time, Bob and I are alone, just the two of us, on the road. Each year, Duane comes less often. Usually he and his family and guests are so quiet, we don't know anyone's there unless we see a car. Once or twice a year, Duane comes up our path to say hello. He admires our flowers. I've often thought I'd like to give him some cuttings, offer to help him start a garden. Perhaps one day I will, if he ever spends enough time here to maintain one.

Passing the house I still think of as Jim's, we stop to chat with our new neighbor, Ralph, who's standing in the driveway looking at the sky. He's taking a break, he tells us, from dismantling a wall to get at a leaky pipe. "There must have been forty pounds of nails in there," he booms. "Every three inches into the studs—and big ones! With everything I keep hearing about what a genius mechanically brilliant guy this was—I don't want to intrude on anyone's sensitive feelings—on Duane's great love and affection for this wonderful, wonderful man —but he fucked up!"

He asks where we're off to, and we tell him.

"If we're not back by tomorrow, call out the ranger," I say, as we head up the road. But I'm confident that if we were to get lost—and of course we won't—Ralph, a lifelong hunter who's never fired a shot on his own land, as far as I know, would track us down himself.

Along much of the road, things are green again. Blackberries and other indomitable shrubs are flourishing. And there are wildflowers: goldenrod, white flat-topped asters and a few purple ones today; earlier in the season, daisies, black-eyed Susan, swamp candle, milkweed.

"The land heals itself well," Bob remarks to me, not for the first time.

I don't respond. Though Bob and I are in accord on most things regarding the landscape, to me, this land looks like it's having a hard life.

It's twenty-six months since the loggers moved on, those hard-working local men Ernie Martin hired in the last year of his life. Two winters, two springs, three summers. Beyond the colorful fringe of greenery along the roadside, only a torn veil of trees blocks the patchy, mangled forest from full view. Even where the coverage is most complete, an atmosphere of disorder and confusion reigns. Pristine wilderness is anything but tidy. But here, wherever I look, limbless trunks stand moribund, or lean, hopeless, against the living, shortening *their* lives. Some of the dead are snapped nearly in two, with great gaping cracks ragged as broken celery, their crowns poised to meet the forest floor. And there are the headers, two big cleared foyers into the forest, where the loggers stacked their harvest and loaded their huge trucks. While the smaller header is verdant with wild grasses, the larger one remains inexplicably barren and brown. Beyond the headers and the trees that line the road, the inner forest is scarred by ruts and gullies two and three feet deep, and false trails that stop abruptly in the churned earth. In hilly places, sometimes flat ones, too, ruts self-perpetuate, filling with water whenever it rains, dispersing the rich upper layers of soil in which new plants might establish themselves, thus maintaining a discontinuity that may be logging's most profound legacy. Such breaks in dense forest disrupt migration patterns of plants and animals, and make the habitat less hospitable to many of its creatures, large and small—including me.

Deep, dark, dense, unbroken, too vast for my mind to fully contain—this is the wilderness that stirs me to the core. So I remain stubborn in my differing opinion. But I'm forced to recognize this: Where I see scars, others are impressed by the grace and swiftness of the road's recovery.

Do I lack appropriate faith in the capacity of the forest for self-renewal? A few years ago, I copied these words from Taoist Huanchu Daoren in my journal: "Mountain forests are beautiful places, but once you become attached to them, they become cities." Jim Harrison, the author who quoted them, defined attached as "a desperate clinging, an obsessiveness that finally blinds you to the wilderness before you, at which point you might as well be in Times Square or the Pentagon."

I miscopied, wrote "bind" for "blind" and spent a long time pondering the phrase until I chanced to return to the original. I decided that, either way, it meant more or less the same well-known thing: obsessive attachment blights the freedom of both possessor and possessed. Indeed, this is the opposite of what I want. I need an openness in every part of myself, even the part that is afraid, to meet the capacious forest. I want to see it for what it is. Mine is a more mature love now. The time is past for the naivete of fantasy and blind desire with which I first ventured beyond the tame edges of the natural world. I want the presence to attend the new in each moment, and I'd wish for both elasticity and rigor as I consider the seemingly endless permutations of what I see.

Nonetheless, out of old habit or perversity or a nagging conviction I can't argue away, when I walk this road my mind lingers on what's been lost.

As I take in the empty spaces, the sad stumps, the crags and snags —all the images of brokenness—I mourn the huge, straight trees and the forest in its wholeness.

Time is what it will take to bring these woods from what I see today back to the wild serenity into which Bob and I wandered on that midsummer evening five years ago. More time than I have. Because most trees grow slowly and have long lives, catastrophes, man-made or natural, leave their mark on the forest for a hundred years or more.

Now and then, I look out the living room window at our small wooded hillside and imagine the land bare. Like the body under the clothes it's all there already, of course. Picture any forest without the trees: it's like envisioning a person naked, someone you know, but with whom you are not so intimate and don't want to be, whose nakedness in the mind's eye is no more erotic than an X-ray. But this is not an apt analogy. The trees are not the clothing of the forest. They are both its superstructure and its infrastructure. And as they shape the landscape, logging reshapes it. But of course, nature, too, reshapes it every day in countless ways, subtle, dramatic, beautiful, violent— sometimes all of these at once, in an instant.

July 1995. A Friday evening. Hot, in the low 80s, an evening temperature as unlikely as snow in July, which is on record here—and absolutely still. Finishing our supper at the picnic table, Bob and I pondered an inscrutable sky. I would have curled up with a novel about then, but at a little past nine it wasn't light enough to read out- side, and I was reluctant to go in. The coolest moments of a summer day tend to linger in the dry old logs of our cabin's walls, and we'd never wanted for a comfortable night's sleep. But we hadn't known an evening here as close and airless as this one.

"Why don't we sleep outside?" I suggested. No rain was predicted. We could set up a tent. Better: we could throw sleeping bags on the floor of our half-built studio up the hill. The walls and roof had gone up yesterday; the windows had not yet arrived. Bob rejected the idea, and as it turned out, we slept well. Pounding rain woke us at first light. Without moving, we glanced out the windows that face our bed at the big pines and balsams thrashing like palms in a hurricane, exclaimed to each other ("Look at that!" "Holy shit!") and, uncharacteristically, went right back to sleep.

An hour later, we awoke to brilliant blue sky, sunlight and calm. I stumbled into the windowless kitchen, hit the light switch. No light. No phone, either. Outside, we saw right away that a fifty-foot balsam at the edge of the lawn had crashed down the high bank into the stream, but a quick tour revealed no other casualties to our woods. It wasn't until we drove to town on the first of our planned errands that we began to sense the extent of the damage. Three men in yellow slickers stood in the intersection, diverting traffic back down the road we'd come from, but no, you couldn't go far that way, either. We got our mail, bought milk at the general store, and went home. There was nowhere else to go: every major road in the area was obstructed by fallen trees.

It wasn't a hurricane, weather officials asserted. And it wasn't a tornado. First, it was referred to as "a microburst." Eventually, someone defined the storm as a *derecho,* an uncommon meteorological phenomenon akin to a tornado, but without the twisting wind currents. It's a line of many thunderstorms that moves as one, propelled by a powerful wall of wind to barrel straight across a relatively narrow path. The word comes from the Spanish for "straight ahead." Swaths of mature, healthy trees—in some places no more than a few feet wide, in others covering acres—lay toppled like pick-up-sticks. Dozens of people were stranded in wilderness areas because the trails or waterways on which they'd entered the forest were obstructed, choked or obliterated by the windthrow. Several campers in two tame state campgrounds, a hundred miles apart, were crushed to death by trees that fell on tents. Within twenty minutes, an estimated ten million trees were toppled over an area about the size of Rhode Island.

In the wake of destruction came controversy: The lumber and paper companies were eager to buy up the downed trees, as they had been after a 1950 hurricane known as "The Big Blowdown," and of course such a purchase would help with the state's huge bill for the clean-up. Conservationists were divided. Whatever else wilderness may mean, it's a legal term in the Adirondacks, and to clean up that part of the mess that lay in the lands labeled "Forest Preserve" would defy the State's constitution which, more than a century ago, designated the Preserve "forever wild." Let nature take its course? Wouldn't all the dead and dying limbs on the forest floor result in wildfire? What about the miles of hiking trails obstructed, the rivers clogged, the canoe carries and wilderness campsites buried under tons of wood? What would best serve the recovery of the vegetable world? Would this also serve the birds and insects and mammals and reptiles and amphibians, the hikers and hunters and research scientists and recent transplants and five-generation natives and assorted other humans— all the animal life of the Adirondack forest community?

I can certainly understand the impulse to clean things up. As anyone unlucky enough to have lived with me will attest, I'm not a particularly tidy person by upbringing, habit or temperament; yet I look around a forest and want to rearrange it. Move that blowdown, trim that dead branch, pick up all those sticks and get them off the trail. Obviously, there's a contradiction here. Wild land is untidy land. Still, though Bob and I say we want our own six acres wild, when trees fall, which they often do, given the preponderance of shallow-rooted balsams, we cut them up and cart them away.

After the derecho, the constitution eventually prevailed, with this compromise: The state would clear out only what was necessary to reopen established waterways and trails. The rest of the forest was left to fend for itself.

"Environmental disharmonies," botanist E. H. Ketchledge calls the forces, swift and slow, that are at any given moment altering the green world everywhere. Cycles of insect invasion. fungal attacks, too much wet or too much dry, for a mere instant by geological measure, can readily kill. Beavers, porcupines, ants, and a variety of tunneling rodents are all adept at re-engineering the landscape. No year passes without impact on some species or some niche of the forest community. The proverbial balance of nature, says Ketchledge, "is more truthfully an episodic teeter-totter."

Though the notion persists in me that we live in a place that has changed relatively little since the first large group of settlers came here from famine-stricken Ireland shortly before our Civil War, I remind myself that this road has nonetheless known its share of change. Like every country road, it is a palimpsest of layered time.

I once talked to a woman about my age who remembers when our road bisected a single farm. Just beyond the bridge, where Jim later built his house, there was pasture from which you could see due south for nine miles to another farm, the one where this woman grew up. As if expanding on this point, Herman brings a snapshot he took from the bridge when he was eight years old. On a bare bank stands our cabin, naked to the road, devoid of any of the trees that now cozy and conceal it all year long. There are no big trees at all in this picture. Which means that the tallest of the trees at our end of the road—trees I'd regarded as my elders—are younger than I.

Land in transition. In the parlance of scientific neutrality, that's how these woods along the road would be designated. And so the stricken earth—assaulted by fire, storm, or human endeavor— is usually described, as if the healthy forest were not, like any community, like the human body, cell by cell, always changing, even as we perceive it as constant. Whatever the source of the assault, "in transition" means this: the sun brings light and warmth to ground it hasn't touched in years. Gloomy corridors in which only the odd shaft of sunlight reached the forest floor become bright glades where, if water and soil conditions are right, light-starved plants can flourish.

The first plants to "enrich" disturbed ground tend to be opportunistic, tough survivors that can tolerate poor soil and other shabby conditions. These pioneers include some of everyone's favorite natives, notably the white birch, *Betula papyrifera,* alabaster lady of the forest, that spring from among the millions of seeds that await such a chance in the soil of a dark wood. But soon the natives have competition: aliens, exotics, escapes—plants that conservationists fret over the way political conservatives fret over certain immigrant groups, blaming them for consuming resources barely adequate to meet native needs, taking up space, making demands beyond what they return, at worst, turning against the community. Unlike their human counterparts, however, alien plants have no predators, no competition, no diseases —all things the natives must battle—to keep their numbers in check.

Far from being a botanical purist, I have a weakness for aliens. I love the aggressive opportunist called purple loosestrife that lines summer's roadsides with flashy swords of color. I'm grateful I don't have as many enemies as this plant does. The state of Vermont has outlawed its propagation, and some field guides have dropped the mantle of objectivity to label it a "noxious weed." I don't know if I fell for it because of its name or the way its stalky inflorescence sets off a wild bouquet. (I'm in good company: Charles Darwin was infatuated with it, too.) Perhaps my secret urge to harbor this illegal dates back to a steamy morning in a Manhattan slum when I was about twenty-two. The man I madly loved and would eventually marry had just sipped a dose of LSD in a glass of orange juice. He looked at me—I, as usual, sober as the day I was born—and said I was pulsating with purple light. Ever since, purple has been my color. And loose? Well, I'd like to be. Strife? Guilty, sir. Of causing it, feeling it, perpetuating it.

I haven't seen any purple loosestrife in our area, despite the fact that it's alleged to be taking over the world. Incorrigible and unrepentant, I've been wanting to transplant some for years. As an ornamental, it was brought to North America in the early 1800s from the European gardens where it was a respected citizen. It's likely some seeds worked their way over by accident, as well. Where purple loosestrife becomes established, it crowds out the natives and usurps their habitat. And it's not a simple plant-for-plant equation. The natives it starves out—sweet flag or wild iris, for instance—are dinner for wildlife. Few creatures care for a loosestrife meal: the seeds are small, the roots tough. That over two hundred species of insects, including bumblebees, honeybees and numerous butterflies feed on loosestrife's nectar or pollen, that the plant is used in some way by forty species of birds, plus some mammals, amphibians and spiders, is never mentioned by its many adversaries. Nor do they note that, far from taking over all the desirable real estate, the purple stalks are commonly seen shoulder to shoulder with rich stands of cattail, a plant that's a veritable supermarket of wildlife nutrients.

Not an underground invader, loosestrife propagates from wind-carried seeds that form in capsules bunched along the tips of the stems —about one hundred seeds per capsule, up to nine hundred capsules per plant. These sheer numbers, coupled with the exceptional ability of this inedible vegetable to sprout from seed in areas already rich with other plants, have made it a leading villain, indeed a threat widely regarded as second only to habitat destruction in many official versions of the drama of endangered species. Still, if some of its ambitious seeds were to wing their way to to my garden and nestle in, I'd be hard-pressed to chase them away.

It is in the smaller plants, the wildflowers, shrubs and young trees of the understory, that the subtext of the forest lies. The very presence of loosestrife, or a more modest favorite of mine, blue vervain, reveals that the ground underneath is wet and poorly drained, whether it appears soggy or dry at a given moment. The canopy tells one story, the understory another perhaps no more true but probably more significant—the real dirt about what's going on. One piece of the story is "wet" or "dry;" other essentials have to do with mineral underlayers powerfully affected by the loss of decomposing leaves and needles caused by logging.

The importance of subtext was taught to me in the early 1970s when I wrote scripts for daytime dramas (a.k.a. soap operas), and it was my task to create lines that encouraged the audience to read between them. The subtext is literally an under-story. The characters speak in such a way that you know they mean more than they say, and perhaps something very different. Subtext builds layers of meaning, enriches familiar stories with nuance, foreshadowing, suspense.

And so the understory suggests where the forest is headed. What's next in forest succession is not everyone's idea of an exciting plot, but the more I learn, the more interested I become. Beneath mature trees lives a world of vast complexity and profound connections—insect societies, biochemical processes—plants competing with plants with varying degrees of hardiness and aggressiveness. Ours is a minimalist canvas by tropical standards, but even the comparatively mundane forests of the northeast are layered with herbaceous plants, fallen trunks, branches and leaves that support animal life from microbes to moose—and we don't, in fact, know a fraction of logging's impacts on these life cycles and their interdependent responses to events—even in one particular small place like Herman Martin's land up the road or Duane's four acres across the stream.

All is not ugliness.

Over Duane's logged land has grown a kind of scar tissue. The torn brown earth is now gentled by grasses and wildflowers. Duane's debacle is turning into a meadow, and everyone comments on how quickly it's healed itself. Everyone but me.

Go walking in Duane's meadow, and the first thing you see is a seventy-foot ash tree still lying where the derecho left it two years ago, not even taken for firewood. But I have to admit that even up close, this former forest is no longer an open wound. As if nature were whispering "See? See!" I found an abundance of the wildflower known as heal-all, not merely in its usual purple, but in uncommon pink and rare white. There was hairy beardtongue, Indian tobacco and downy lobelia, and even blue vervain.

I don't know as much as I once did about what grows across the stream because it's so hard to walk there. With drainage disrupted by the removal of the trees, there's no level footing: a rickety surface of damp, slippery limbs wobbles over the wet unknown. It's similar to walking in an alder swamp, except that here there's nothing tall enough to prevent seeing where you're going, and nothing to grab hold of if you slip. For all I know, this meadow could be home to many plants small and rare. Fields and meadows have understories, too: tiny plants secreted in the shade of goldenrods and tall grasses. Left naked to the sun's embrace, disturbed ground can be profoundly fertile.

I'd hoped to see some fireweed, a tall, magenta-panicled wild-flower that often flourishes in land that logging has scraped raw. Fireweed towers over most other wildflowers, so it's easy to spot from afar, and after a cursory investigation, I know there's none at Duane's, though I don't know why. Its preferred habitat is "disturbed ground," say my field guides. Belying the boldness of its color, it rises with a lacey fragility of form. Its four-petaled florets resemble those of old-fashioned garden phlox, but the cultivar's brightest blush is meek by comparison. Though to my senses phlox has a perfume much finer and more intense, fireweed's brilliant florets produce quantities of nectar so valued by honey-makers that, in the Pacific Northwest, both bees and apiarists follow logging operations, moving every few years to newer cuts where the plant is most abundant.

Despite my disappointment about the absence of fireweed, I can't help noticing that Duane's forest is starting over. Here and there,

shin-high cedars, balsams, maples, even oaks, bask in the unobstruct-
ed sun. It's possible that I may see trees across the stream again.

Many people would consider this a happy ending. I withhold
judgement.

Whether Duane's land is ugly or beautiful is not the point, any
more than the fact that his logging spoiled our view.

What's important is that disturbing the ground by disturbing the
trees disturbs everything—birds like the ovenbird and the redstart
whose ground-born fledglings need the depth of a mature forest to
shield them from prey, salamanders that need the leaflitter that decid-
uous trees replenish year after year, big cats that are simply shy. On the
other hand, opening the field of view helps hawks and owls to flour-
ish, replete with warbler, rabbit, rodent. And, like Sleeping Beauty,
some things in the forest—among them, the seeds of the paper birch—
want to be disturbed. How to weigh the pluses and the minuses?
There are tens of thousands of microorganisms we don't know the first
thing about. Which plants do you choose between? Which birds?
Which mammals? Loosestrife or pipsissewa? Ovenbird or hawk? Tax-
paying man or secretive lynx?

Is one species more important than another? Being of an egalitari-
an bent, I was surprised to learn that the answer appears to be yes.
There are certain species that apparently hold all the other life of the
community together. They are not necessarily the ones that dominate
in either size or number in a given place, but might be small or rare,
and attract little notice until they disappear. These are called keystone
species and without them, things fall apart. This means large numbers
of other species vanish from a region. Scientists are just beginning to
investigate how many species an ecosystem can lose before the impact
is felt in the disruption of large-scale processes that revitalize soil,
moderate weather and water cycles, and keep diseases in check. In
most places, keystone species have yet to be identified, and no one
knows which species are the most important to protect.

There is no question, however, that one thing logging often kills along with trees is a group of fungi called mycorrhizae (the source of truffles in some parts of Europe) on which the forest depends. We have no truffles, of course, but when I stick my spade into the soil beneath one of our balsams, I meet resistance from a substance quite unlike any other I've ever encountered. The dense, damp, ash-colored mat could be mistaken, perhaps, for some strange, underground moss. In fact, it's an intricately woven network of tiny filaments that are attached to the tree's roots. Virtually all conifers rely on such a network for part of their nourishment. Balsam and mycorrhizae are mutually dependent partners of a symbiotic pair. The tree provides the fungi with sugar made by photosynthesis, and in turn, the fungi's far-reaching filaments serve as an extension of the tree's root system, increasing its access to nutrients from the soil. Neither one can survive without the other.

When the mycorrhizae are scraped away by the heavy equipment used in logging, the acidic soil in which conifers thrive turns alkaline, becoming more hospitable to grasses than to most of our native trees. The forest floor is no longer suitable for a forest. Any seedlings that germinate will die after a few years. Only time will tell if that has happened here. Only time will tell what will become of Duane's new trees if they do survive. If they grow to block the view from his new living room, still unbuilt, he may cut them down again.

13

I once read that every Adirondack story has logging in it. I never thought it would be true of mine.

When we first bought the cabin, we gave less thought to the building itself than to its setting and what the surrounding woods hid and revealed: stream, road, bridge, sky, and of course Duane's house. It never occurred to us that Duane might cut down his trees, nor did we consider the obvious fact that our own trees would grow—to block a water view, limit the light that enters the house, shorten daylight on the lawn.

For the most part, nature's changes, like the processes of our bodies and minds, are invisible. Sometimes, if you happen to be looking, you can catch that dazzling moment when the sun breaks through the air on a cloudy morning, changing the sky from gray to blue and with it the colors of everything, including human moods. You can watch the snow melt, but no matter how closely you look, you can't see flowers grow, or watch the shoots burst from the earth. You can watch the leaves drift toward the ground, but you never see them turn russet or gold before they fall. You think you watch your children grow, but you never really see it. Invisibly, children grow. So do trees.

Bob and I know we argue too much, and we often catch ourselves bickering about trees. There are several trees on our lawn that have been in contention for years, particularly one tall balsam that has risen and spread to fill Bob's sky, disrupt his cosmos, and defeat our garden with its shade.

I don't want to live in a dark spot. Though I take a special comfort in the shelter of deep woods, I love sunlight and open space as much as anyone. Still, I balk at taking the life of a beautiful healthy tree. If our survival depended on our garden's yield, it would be different. It would be different even if we could use the tree. But we can't burn balsam for heat—too resinous—or mill it for boards, or build with the logs. Though there are some balsams in our old walls, they are less resistant to insects and other log-house predation than the cedars of which the cabin is primarily made.

"I think of tree-removal as weeding, only on a larger scale," Bob likes to say.

I tell him I'd consider cutting the balsam if it could somehow be used. If we cut it around Thanksgiving time, perhaps, and arranged to give it to some poor family in the city as a Christmas tree? Or made a plan to use the logs for a carport or woodshed?

"Maybe we could do that," says Bob without much interest.

I know he's chafing at the bit to cut that tree, and doesn't want to wait. Still, for now at least, I hold out.

As I think about all the stories and understories and mortal struggles of my relatively simple forest, one idea continues to assert itself: "No matter how awful or insignificant, how ugly or beautiful, everything in the bush has its own right to be there. No one can challenge this right unless compelled by some necessity of life itself." Laurens van der Post said this of the South African bush. The wilderness, he went on, would always forgive the impositions of necessity, but only those—and would know the difference.

Necessity is a concept I understand. It is a guidepost that, for better or worse, has been with me since I was born into a working-class family that never shook the constraints of wartime scarcity. When I asked my father for something, *necessity* was the criteria by which he said yes or no. In the way that adolescent and parental values often diverge, my father's idea of necessity was usually at odds with mine. The things he decided I didn't need ranged from a felt skirt appliquéd with poodles, like the skirts every other girl wore in fifth grade, to a college education. Not that he didn't believe in education. But, at seventeen, I had a good job. I didn't need to go to college.

Though in this and many other things I successfully defied him,

I've not only perpetuated the criteria of necessity upon myself in good times and lean, I've made a virtue of both the discipline and the deprivation they foster, priding myself on absurdities like my ability to enjoy a stale crust of bread.

Equally absurd, I've considered myself virtuous for not wanting a fine house. Now Bob and I agree it's time to improve the cabin a bit, and questions of necessity lurk at my shoulder. Is that why I hesitate? I am filled with trepidation.

Nonetheless, we've set a start date with the talented young builder who put up our studio, a simple 12' x 16' wooden structure on a hill overlooking the stream. Its construction was one of those rare, felicitous projects about which Bob and I were in complete agreement. We will argue over how to correct the insufficient light over the dining room table, over whether to battle or acquiesce to a grasshopper invasion, over the shortest distance between two points. But we never argued about the need for a private work space, where it should go, what it should be. Even sharing its use has been easy; we never want to be there at the same time. The studio was my idea and more or less my design—though it was only after I began to write there that I realized how much I needed it. Now, at the beginning of each summer when I open its six windows and take my seat on the small deck overlooking the stream, I feel like my creative center has awakened from its winter sleep.

Even with the studio, however, the cabin is too small. We've always intended to add on to it. After seeing how our builder turned Jim's hovel into a showplace filled with pale, warm lemony light for its new owners, we decided it's time. An addition will permit such amenities as closets, a basement, a better bathroom, a larger bedroom, a wood stove for more efficient, self-reliant heat. Yet it seems frightening and radical to make these changes.

The cabin, simple as a wooden tent, has grown around me like a skin. I feel this most profoundly when I spend extended periods here alone. When Bob and I are here together, it is a skin we share. This little place, with all the solitudes and friendships it's nurtured, is part of the cement that binds us.

No wonder the prospect of changing it has filled my dreams with alien invaders.

For more than thirty years, I've had two kinds of recurring dreams about houses. In one, alone in a house with small children, I am trapped by marauders: strong young men, a construction crew. They are moving fast, let no one and nothing get in their way. I pick up a phone to call for help, but all the wires have been cut. They have a van outside, and are taking away all the furniture, everything.

Last night, as Bob and I sat in a roadside diner eating hot turkey sandwiches I looked out the window and saw a convoy of flatbed trucks passing on the road, huge ones, loaded with building supplies, and I shuddered at all those remembered dreams. By ordering construction done in my house, I acquiesce to the occupation of my dreams and that terrifying helplessness.

In the other dream, however, I discover a room where I live—it's usually my apartment—that I never knew existed. Awash in golden sunlight, full of thrilling surprise, it opens up my world.

Despite my fears, I want to change the cabin. I still have far to go, but my time here has begun to teach me that things can change, and yet the center can hold.

Last fall, to match the original log walls, we carefully selected some forty northern white cedars, *arbor vitae,* to be harvested from various parts of our land. Now the builder has decided the addition will require more than he originally estimated. And so it happens that the logging part of my story is not just about lumbering done by others, but also about timber cutting in which I participate.

No more live trees will be cut; they'd still be too green next spring when the construction is to begin, and we'd have to put off building

for another year. But this summer, much of our time in the woods—
our own woods, my brother's, Herman's—is spent scouting cedars,
down or dead. Scanning the forest as I walk, I spot them like familiar
faces in a huge Grand Central Station crowd. In fact, I find myself
evaluating every dead tree for its potential in either a wall or a fire in
the stove.

I've also learned that some men love to cut down trees, including
the men I love who love the forest best.

Walking up a steep hill into my brother's woods in Paradox to join
Jerry and Bob, I round a bend and see the two of them from a distance.
They are cutting up some hardhack, a dense tree with a rough golden
bark and a slender trunk, perfect for the small stove we've chosen. Bob
and Jerry are close friends, but there's a special bond between men
who cut wood together—in part, perhaps, because it is largely a word-
less operation, and in part because it is dangerous. You can plan and
strategize about a cut, but once the noisy saw is pumped into action,
speech can't be heard above the din. So you must be well-attuned to
your partner—all the more so because your life may depend on him.
Large-scale logging is in its third century on this continent, and more
lumbermen still die on the job in a typical year than American work-
ers in any other occupation.

Logging is a major theme of the folklore and songs of the
Adirondacks and the rest of the Great North Woods. Some of those
songs are romantic and enthusiastic work songs, others are moving
dirges for young men lost in the treacherous river drives of the nine-
teenth century, or the sudden drop of a huge tree in the forest. For the
addition to the cabin, Bob and Jerry and Herman have hauled out logs
about twenty feet long. When we cut firewood, we bring it out in a
pick-up truck in stove-sized chunks. This small-scale, selective cutting
of dead or down trees and the occasional live one doesn't involve all
the heavy equipment, road-carving and erosion of a full-scale logging
operation, nor is it usually as dangerous. Still, falling timber can strike

and kill anyone working in the woods.

As I approach Bob and Jerry, I feel a quickening of eagerness to join them. And I realize this feeling is intensified by the visceral smell of chain saw oil mixed with the resins of fresh-cut green wood that I once associated with the death of the forest. Now these unquestionably polluting vapors evoke the pleasures of spending time in the beautiful live woods with the people I love.

I love the feel of the logs in my hands, the strength and stretch of my body as I hoist them into the truck, and, yes, even that pungent green smell. Cutting timber in Paradox has become a kind of family fun, something we might choose, even on a perfect hiking day, over climbing a mountain. Rosemary and I frequently join the men, though our role is limited to fetching tools now and then, piling brush, helping to load the truck.

We all take such pleasure in this hard work, in getting very, very dirty, sweaty, thirsty, hot. There's satisfaction in both cleaning up the woods, and in staying warm with wood you've cut and hauled and stacked yourself. We profess to enjoy physical labor much more than our own diverse occupations. In the sun-dappled woods, teaching, writing, systems management, medical research, all pale compared to growing vegetables, making furniture, clearing land, moving stones. We all feel we could relish these tasks day in, day out. Yearn for downward mobility. I know that many Adirondackers who work outdoors have a good stock of complaints about the way they earn a living. But I've never met one who longed for someone else's indoor job in some other place.

Devotion to trees. That's what was said of Ernie Martin in his eulogy. In the years since his death, I've come to understand that I must reconcile the disturbance I feel in the face of logging with the idea that some loggers can be lovers of trees, that they do, in fact, care for the forest. Who am I to say that I love the forest better than the hunter or the logger, or in the only right or true way? I'm ashamed that

I once believed the person who works the land loves it less than one who merely walks it.

I never imagined I could change so much. Or have I?

I think about the fact that our house is essentially *all* trees reorganized into different form—from log walls and pine floors to birch-bark panels (a tree's tube of skin split and stretched to a plane) to the parchment lampshade, all our books and papers, the inlaid footstool, the fire's warmth. If every tree is a spirit, how many spirits in the fire?

More than I fret over the uncertain fate of Bob's offending balsam, I am troubled by the living trees that will be displaced by the fact of our new construction. No trees grow where the new room will be, but several brush against the as-yet-imaginary roof and far wall, and their roots spread through the sandy soil that will be excavated for the foundation. The forty foot oak, struggling with disease and weather damage here at the northernmost end of its range, must go a bit before its time. And the fine young white pine, the brambles, the scruffy balsams—it's so easy to rationalize human necessity.

What's the difference between want and need? We define these terms pretty much as we please.

In the bush, van der Post said, "there is always…an eye upon you, even if it is only the eye of some animal, bird, reptile or little insect, recording in its own way in the book of life how you carry yourself. And…the plants, the grasses, the leaves of the trees and the roots of all growing things…. They, too, shake with the shock of our feet and vibrate to the measure of our tread and…have their own ways of regis-tering what we bring or take from the life for which they are a home…."

The chipmunks will surely have an opinion when we cut the oak tree. There is a place under this tree that I call "the chipmunks' garden." Things with berries grow there: bearberry and wintergreen and pipsissewa, low, understory plants with dark, shiny, hard-cuticled leaves. And among the greenery, a few feet from the bird feeder where seeds fall all day, the chipmunks have excavated several entryways to their tunneled homes. These burrows came first; the garden followed, from seed dropped by birds on their way to better things at the feeder, or maybe by the chipmunks themselves, or their competitive, if not downright hostile, neighbors, the red squirrels. In any case, it's through their garden that the chipmunks now bring home the groceries, scurrying with cheeks popping full, into their subterranean pantry. I wonder what it will be like for them if they're sleeping there in hibernation when that oak is cut. It's obvious, as Wendell Berry points out, that even the most ascetic vegetarian must partake of the world, including other species, to survive. But, he says, "If we can't exempt ourselves from use, we must deal with the issues raised by use…we cannot exempt use from care."

When I destroy his home, his food supply, and his garden it makes no difference to the chipmunk that I *care*. Maybe it makes a difference to me.

"The fact is, Bibi," Herman tells me, very gently but with absolute conviction, "you have too many trees."

Herman still visits the farm, cuts the grass, makes basic repairs, but when he comes alone, he doesn't spend the night there anymore; he stays with us and has become an energetic participant in whatever projects may be underway. Our cabin has become Herman's base camp. When occasionally he sojourns at the farm with friends and relatives, it's at the cabin, even in our absence, that they assemble to go up the road. We have encouraged him to make the cabin "his" as he has allowed us to make the farm "ours."

When the three of us are here together, much of our activity is about wood in one way or another. Like his father, Herman is an accomplished woodsman, so it's logical that, with Herman here today to help, this would be a good time to cut that balsam.

"There are so many trees in the Adirondacks," Herman presses on. "Millions and millions." Billions. I guess I am starting to think of trees as if they were people. I'm unconvinced this is so wrong-headed.

I look out the window, change the subject. "It's getting to be time to move the bird feeder. It's smack in the middle of our new bedroom."

"Have you ever tried your bird feeder out in the open?" Herman keeps politicking.

"We don't have very much out-in-the-open," I admit.

"You'd get more birds than you do there in the woods," he continues. "It's too closed in for them." For shy birds? Too closed in?

I see the enthusiasm of pioneers in Bob and Herman as they talk about getting more light in the place and figure out where the tree should fall, and how they'll engineer it. Being human animals, we create a place called home, an endeavor that includes bringing within a shelter's walls what offers comfort, whether that's crystal chandeliers and priceless carpets, or a rough-hewn chair and the light of the outdoors. Do I want to cultivate a garden? Or will I settle, like the chipmunks, for whatever grows, and keep that balsam? Before I know it, I've acquiesced.

The balsam will not become some poor family's Christmas tree. And we're not going to use the logs.

I won't watch. I go up to the studio, planning to work, but end up sitting on the deck listening to the wind and the birds and the stream. I feel like I'm waiting in the wings while a companion animal is euthanized. But this tree isn't being put out of any misery. I feel guilty that I didn't come out more strongly in its defense. Like Bob, I want to improve the chances of the unnecessary flowers we so enjoy. Necessity. I'm treating my beloved garden like art funding in the federal budget. Is it because I was raised to cultivate self-denial that I feel so uneasy? Surely we won't be punished for sacrificing a tree to maintain enough open sky to use a telescope on the lawn by night, and sun a flower bed and a few tomato plants by day. Punished by whom? How? The concept of punishment for taking the life of a tree is ancient and ubiquitous. In some cultures, when people spoke of "ancestral trees" they referred to their own ancestors. Have I really become so primitive?

They're not using a chain saw, so there's no preamble. Crack. One loud snap and it's done. Then a whooshing plop of needles, branches and cones. The balsam's shapely spire lands on the one tiny scrap of lawn I can see from here on top of the hill, just as Bob and Herman are moving the picnic table out of its way.

They couldn't be neater, harm not a twig of anything but their chosen target, cart the remains by great armloads into the woods, leaving just an anthill of sawdust.

Later, Bob counted the rings in the small stump. The tree was thirty-five years old.

PART VI

Coda

*In the traditional world of nomadic tribes,
one departs and returns. The journey is not
linear and permanent...but circular and
continuous. And no...essential journey is
complete until the return is made.*

Ancestral Voice, Charles Woodard

*The Land can speak us back to ourselves, a
kind of autobiography.*

From Where We Stand, Deborah Tall

When you see me smiling, you know I'm lost.
Earl "Fatha" Hines

14

August 20

I wake up one morning and all the birds are different. A hawk screams above the stream. The goldfinches are gone from the feeder. When the sun moves out from behind the Scotch pine that's three times as high as the house, there is no wind. Whatever blew the birds in and out came in the night. Behind the pin cherry, a single cackle, then pecking. A splash in the stream: something is down there. It is only a pair of robins, taking a last icy dip.

Each August, there comes a morning like this, with a palpable freshening in the air, when I can no longer forget that soon I will be trading all this wild space and the kingfisher's great arcing dive, his swoop and rattle, for dark rooms and constant email.

Like the birds, Bob and I still migrate south each fall to make our living. In twelve days, we will return to Manhattan. Perhaps we could no more stay the winter here than the Blackburnian warbler, the cedar waxwing or the ruby-throated hummingbird.

I am, by nature, restless. I like being on the move. This is the one place I have known where I can feel completely alive and whole and content just sitting in a chair. This must be what home means: to paraphrase Eliot, my still point in the turning world.

In summer, that point is not the cabin itself, but the studio. If the studio is my self-portrait, it is modest, yet with its cathedral ceiling, full of aspiration, and less cluttered than any other space I call mine. It contains three pieces of art: a hundred-year-old stained glass window, a Navaho basket decorated with turtles, and a fine Hopi pot. There is another tiny basket on a bookshelf that contains a handful of hickory nuts gathered beneath trees at Faulkner's Mississippi homestead. Outside, surrounding the green trim on the six windows, there's a trace of whimsy in the narrow border of rosy violet that picks up one of the colors in the stained glass. And most important, a small deck over-looking the stream—my favorite place to work. I've chosen to do no landscaping here so there's no weeding or maintenance to distract me.

Inside, the building is unfinished. The floor is plywood, the walls and beams rough pine. It has book shelves, an outlook to three views of the forest. There are two desks, rocking chairs, a music stand. Electricity, but no plumbing and no phone. By day, it is usually my place. Bob works or studies or plays music here at night.

As I lie in bed in the cabin and read, the studio is behind me. Yet the music drifting down from the dark hillside seems to curl around the house to come directly to me through the open window I face. Whether Bob is playing a piece through, or practicing a single passage, the ethereal sounds of his clarinet or flute bathe me in well-being.

In the morning, I often pause on the lawn and look up the path to the studio, a path covered with pine needles, beaten down by my feet, my words, myself. Before we began thinking about the studio, the path wasn't there. Nor did we do any clearing to create it. We simply wore it in over a year or so as we climbed to the top of the small hill to study the site and plan the building. By the time the construction was done, the path had established itself.

Though it's a very short path, it turns as you enter the woods, and winds through the trees so you can't see where it goes. One never knows where the path will lead, no matter how familiar, not the path to the studio, the road to the farm, even the hundred steps or so across the bridge. When I go to the studio to write I have no idea what will happen, what words, what birds or animals will come, whether I will stick to a straight route, or be unable to resist the temptation to write my way down some intriguing but possibly pointless track. Sometimes such a byway will result in great finds, new revelations. It is equally likely to turn into a briar patch with nothing to redeem it, and through which I must pick my way back slowly, having wasted hours, even days.

When I'm on assignment for an editor who cares less about what I say than the number of words I turn in, I've learned to be firm with myself: *Don't go that way. There lies trouble, maybe even the abyss.* With anything I'm writing for its own sake, however, I find these side routes irresistible. Part of me is still rebelling against the unrelenting pressure of writing soaps through the seventies, when I was frequently required to create a half-hour script, final draft, in half a day. So, even though patience is not one of my virtues, I don't mind that it takes me a long time to do good work. For me, writing is part discipline, part day-dream, part finding the shortest distance between two points, part wandering all over the map.

Miraculously, when I'm in my place on this small hill, the discipline usually flows as easily as the dreaming. This makes my path very different from the one I walk in the city, to the desk in the sunniest corner of my apartment. There, writing is work. Here, it's more like play.

It is here that some things have spelled themselves out for me, that the sound of the stream casts a spell. It is here that I'm still able to get lost.

August 21

When I arrive at the studio in the morning, the sun is in the crown of the big birch tree. As we carefully sited this tiny building around the view, I didn't think anything of the fact that, like the cabin, it faces east, the direction of orientation, from the Latin *orior*, to rise up, proceed from a source, become aligned, take one's bearings.

Nor did I realize until the building was finished, that when I sit on the deck in my chosen spot, the glorious white birch is in the very center of my picture. Of a stately height, and broad in the crown, it is the one significant tree on this part of the bank. I can easily imagine this view with no other tree but the birch, stretching its branches to fill the sky. One reason I'm here this morning is to watch it dance in today's extraordinary wind.

This summer, I've learned something that makes me as proud as a six-year-old on her first two-wheeler—though surely the people in the world who can do this must far outnumber those who can't. What I've taught myself is to tell time across the morning by the trees and the sky. Not precise minute-by-minute time, but good enough time for the life I live here: that when the sun sits at the apex of the skinny, one-sided balsam next to the birch, it's somewhere between 9:30 and 9:45. I trace its movement across the morning by the landmarks of my tree-tops. Each day, my feeling grows that, observing the sun, I see a clock. I stop wearing my watch. I know.

If I were here all year, the seasons would change the landmarks of my hours. Would clock become calendar? I'd watch the birch drop its leaves, one by one and by the hundreds in the big gusts, until the sun shines in a moon-white ball through its naked crown. In winter, the lacework of branches and their tiny twigs form synapses only birds can cross between earth and sky. I'd mark spring's beginning when the tips of those fragile branches blush dark red and maybe I'd discover where, in the circle of the birch tree's life, the harmonic of that rosy color can be found. There must be one. The maple buds, brighter, and with more orange than the birch, foretell the blaze of autumn in the roseate glow they bring to spring's palette. Perhaps the birch's anthocyanin, source of the spring fire in all buds, sleeps in the rich terra cotta of the inner bark hidden beneath the papery layers of white.

I think of the night when we were lost, and I sat against a hemlock tree, savoring a rare moment to sit still in the woods, just looking, listening, for whatever the forest might reveal. Now I do that almost every day.

August 22

We have nine more days here. One of Bob's friends who's camping nearby has invited himself and his family over, and Bob of course wants to say yes.

This makes me want to tear my hair out. His, too.

Instead, I stand on the lawn at the edge of the path, listening. It sounds like someone is taking an ax to the studio's metal roof. This is not a dream. It's a squirrel harvesting cones from the tops of the red pines that surround the building. Dropped from a treetop height of sixty feet or more, even a small green cone lands with a resounding thwack. As I step onto the deck, the barrage stops, replaced by an impatient twittering I might attribute to an irritable bird if I didn't know better. *They can't wait for us to leave,* I think. Same with the mice who gather our crumbs by night. Whose forest is it?

If it belongs to whoever is at the top of the food chain, it belongs to the bears. On July 4th at about 9 a.m. I looked up from my weeding to see a large black bear rising to his hind legs, front paws grasping the bottom of the bird feeder, less than a dozen yards from where I stood. The same hefty adult male, I'm sure, that all our neighbors have been chasing from their bird feeders since spring. I wanted Bob, who was in the house, to see him. But when I yelled, "Bear!" the creature, who had no doubt heard something quite like this before, bounded off—not in the greatest haste—up the studio path into the woods.

Some years, for a variety of reasons, bears visit bird feeders, hang out on front porches, roam the towns, make routine runs on restaurant dumpsters, and crop up in every conversation. But old-timers—even tiny, ancient, widows living alone—just shrug their stooped shoulders and say, "They were here before we were."

So, whose forest is it? Once I put out the birdseed, does it belong to the birds or the bears? Whose needs are more important? My need for quiet or my neighbor's pleasure in something that makes an unholy racket? Bob's need for the North Star, my love of the tree? Bob's need for company, mine for solitude? "Balance" is a buzzword for navigating through rough passes in any relationship, but as

Ketchledge says of the so-called balance of nature, what you actually live with is "an episodic teeter-totter" in constant flux.

This is the time of year Bob and I argue about houseguests. It's a perennial conflict that Bob is on vacation in the summer, and, for the most part, I am not.

Keeping an open door to our home is deep in Bob's generous nature: anyone can come, anytime. No worry about how or what to feed them, what we'll do.... It will take care of itself. In this, I'm glad that over the years I've become more like him and less like I was when I lived with my ex-husband in the Hamptons, where entertaining is a competitive sport. And I've grown less like my mother, who rarely had guests because she believed her house wasn't nice or clean enough. Still, my style requires a clean house with lots of food in it, and planned meals. Sometimes I love to cook fancy meals. But in the past two weeks we've had three different sets of overnight guests. This makes me feel like I'm running a hotel.

Today, I suggest a compromise Bob is happy to meet: he won't invite his friends for dinner, but for a burger lunch he'll cook on the lawn. Then he'll take them all on a hike, leaving me in peace. We congratulate ourselves on solving this one without a fight.

We're more likely to have bad fights in the pressure cooker of the city but, even in a house that could have been the model for the Log Cabin Syrup label, we don't live an idyll.

For reasons variously known or unknown to me, Bob can fall into dark moods that can last an hour or persist like a long spell of bad weather. Sometimes the most trivial things will set him off: he'll buy something that needs to be assembled, refuse to read the instructions, become frustrated that it doesn't work, and angry at the world. When this happens I may get angry at him, though I try to ignore it. Bob complains I'm too quick to criticize. "You have an edge," he says. "You constantly have this edge and it's the same for every little minor thing."

It's true, I'm rough-cut lumber, uneven and a little sharp. Quick tempers run in my family. When Bob thinks, rightly or wrongly, that he sniffs criticism, he shuts down and stands off in the posture of a snail. This drives me to emotional extremes that serve only to solidify his position. He'll dart out of his shell just long enough to finish my sentences for me, hoping to deflect some imaginary blow. Invariably he gets it wrong, which makes me still angrier.

I tell myself, *keep your mouth shut, you crabby thing. Scolding, ranting, raving. How sick I know he is of the sound of my voice. Croaking like a raven. I'll pay for it, too, will feel miserable when communication and everything else between us is terrible for the rest of the day and night.*

In these tense periods, we twirl in circles, getting nowhere, picking and pecking at each other's words. Our lives become airless, a closed system. I'm not sure if the way out is always the same, or unique to each battle. But I know that we always lose sight of the pleasure we get out of the life we've made together.

Our last houseguest told us over dinner about the disagreements, disappointments, frustrations and misunderstandings that had recently resulted in his parting ways with a woman he'd been with for three years. As he described his own less than exemplary behavior and that of his partner, Bob and I nodded in recognition, and in turn commented,

"I do that sometimes," or, "We've had that problem, too."

Our friend replied, "I guess with us there was just no bedrock. When we'd have one of these fights, everything would just fall through the floor."

We had to acknowledge that this doesn't happen to us. However deeply we stray into squabbling, there is always a point of return.

This year I am in the middle of a project I could just as easily continue here. I choose to go back because home is where Bob is. Yes, he's a curmudgeon, and he is difficult enough that I have more than once—as what mated person hasn't?—tried to imagine life without him. This fantasy fades quickly when I realize that I can't bear to think of witnessing the coming of spring without his company. We've both spent time alone in the cabin. We look forward to these separations. For me, a week apart is great. A month is an endurance test.

At times, I've thought of our relationship as a wild river rising from the heart of the mountain forest. At times tumultuous or joyous, at times dry, empty and narrow, at times placid and flowing, but always in motion. We've created a good life together despite the dry spots and the rapids and the long carries.

August 23

I am invisible today.

As light filters through leaves and branches that shift with every breath of wind among old trees, the parameters of visibility are in constant flux. So many places to hide. So many shadows, creating and dissolving new spaces in an eyeblink. And, over time, of course, as the trees and shrubs secretly grow, familiar shadow patterns change almost unnoticed, the way the balsam grew to shade our garden. One can walk the same path daily, even at the same hour, and see something different each time—not necessarily because something different is there. It was in this way that I discovered the wild thyme that marked the beginning of my friendship with Jim, and just last month, a few yards down the road from where the thyme grows, I suddenly saw an old apple tree for the first time, as if, in all its hoary age, it had miraculously appeared where there was only alder and scrubby pine before. Each spring, creamy blossoms show me more wild apple in the neighborhood. But until that July night, I knew of none on our land. Why did I see it at that moment? In all the hundreds of times I'd passed the tree, it was never at such an hour, nearly ten, never under quite that sky, still light enough to identify an apple tree in the last moments of the long northern twilight.

Sometimes, as every hunter and birdwatcher knows, what you see depends on not being seen. But I can't explain why, out in the open, I am more or less visible on different days, at different times.

Suddenly, almost at my fingertips, there's a chickadee in the small cherry tree that shades my chair. This bird is so light, it hangs upside down on a thin oval leaf less than an inch wide and two inches long. Moments later, a squirrel skitters the length of the deck, nearly grazing my foot. Now a swallowtail butterfly lands on the table six inches from my knee. These are among the most familiar creatures of my world. That they pay me no more attention than they do the furniture makes me as ridiculously happy as if this chickadee were the Elegant Trogon birders travel half way around the world to add to their life lists.

The chickadee is the most common bird in my environs, and it is the one to which I pay the least attention. I am always listening for the distant trills of some warbler I will never see, while every day the chickadee sings in my trees, sounding cheer in desolate winter, announcing spring, sharing the feeder with summer's fickle migrants.

"Oh, it's just a chickadee," I often hear myself saying after following some elusive avian through the woods. *Oh, it's just Bob....* He came up the path a moment ago to tell me he's going into town. Can I recall the color of the shirt he's wearing? Of course not.

There are days when Bob comes home from work and astonishes me by saying, "It's so nice to see you." And I think, *Why? It's only me. I'm always here.* Other times I feel, with greater or lesser distress, depending on my mood, that he's no more aware of me than he is of the furniture.

Live with anyone long enough, and inevitably you take refuge in some blind spots—spots that may feel more like acreage, sometimes an entire country.

There are periods when I feel we are like closed books side by side on a shelf. Conversely, sometimes I feel he knows so well what I'm thinking that there's no point in speaking. This is both profoundly satisfying and mildly annoying. And it is a tribute to him—though it can frustrate me no end—that in many ways I find him ever more mysterious and complex. There are secret places in his heart that I still long to reach.

With Bob, and in most other parts of my life, I prefer to be seen. In the forest, the more invisible I am, the more welcome I feel. Ignored by other creatures, I'm assured we make little enough impact that the forest goes about its business. I worry that this will change when our house is larger and the patch of woods between the house and the studio a few trees smaller.

How invisible would I become if I stayed here alone? What wonders I'd see! Already, I've replaced Jim, become keeper of the road, its royal mistress. There would be days when, with the sound of light wind, or one distant small bird and a remote insect thrum, I would happily be just the human animal—one species of many, never alone in the forest. Other days, I'd be as lonely as Jim was and twice as crazy.

August 24

Will I have to skip making jam this year? To go back to the city leaving millions of ripening blackberries would feel like ignoring Thanksgiving or Christmas. Last August, I was surrounded by steam and jars, my eyes savoring the luster of the simmering berries, my elbows aching from stirring the kettle. If I were making jam today, the bear wouldn't have been scarfing down birdseed in our yard again last night.

We saw him from the living room window at dusk. Bob opened the screen door and stood out on the stoop, berating him mildly, as if he were an unruly student. "That's not yours. You can't have that. Go away now!"

He was a beautiful, healthy-looking bear, with a glossy midnight coat and light brown snout. We'd never had such a close, long look at a bear, and we were enthralled. This is stupid, I thought suddenly, and saying so, I yanked Bob inside, and closed the heavy wooden door. In the dark house, we gaped from the windows as the bear trotted into the woods with the tubular glass-and-metal feeder in his mouth. He dropped the feeder on the path. Then he came back to the lawn to lick up what he'd spilled along the way. He's really hungry, I thought. Even indoors, I felt a little vulnerable.

"He could rip through a screen in a second if he wanted to," I said. "Maybe we should close the windows?"

Bob was busy trying to take a picture of the animal and didn't answer. We didn't close the windows, and the bear, having eaten every last sunflower seed, bounded off into the woods. With all his impressive heft, he was silent and graceful as a cat.

If the berries were ripe, this bear would have been feasting on them, deep in the woods. Day by day, we've scarcely gathered enough to toss into our breakfast cereal. The summer's been a fairly dry one, hot in July, cool in August. We've had a lot of rain in the two days since I checked my favorite berry patch. There's more rain to come. But I don't know if what the fruit needs now is water or sun, warmth or coolness, or if the berries, as sometimes happens, won't ripen at all but just dry up into hard little embroidery knots no creature will eat. Jim would know. All the forces at work along this road were, like the chipmunks he fed and the woodchucks on which he waged chemical warfare, his intimates. No one will ever taste his truest secrets.

Yet I'm convinced that, with all his boastful talk and clandestine hoarding, Jim didn't tell lies. Nor do I believe it was a kind of lie that everyone knew different parts of him, or that one part was more or less true than another. Surely Helen knew something her children didn't. Otherwise why would she have spent every Friday with him for fifteen years, and driven 1500 miles with him on a week's vacation? On the other hand, I don't doubt that he was the cruel stepfather who took advantage of his wife's children and victimized the family with his packrat perversities: surely this man Helen's daughters described was real. Nor was there dissembling in his paternal affection for Duane, or his loyalty and friendship to us. These were as plain as the truth of his house. The one big falsehood he did tell—to me and Bob, to Duane, to all his local friends and enemies, every day with his boastful manner and his twinkling eyes—was that he was *just fine*.

This morning I picked our breakfast berries from bushes I'd always thought of as his. In Jim's day, I made sure he'd done all the picking he cared to before I went out, though he'd tell me he had no more right to them than I. But, by way of asserting that he and I had first picking rights over others, he once warned me he'd seen outsiders on the road, getting out of trucks with their arms full of flats. "They didn't get nothin'. Too early. But you go get them berries tomorrow," he instructed me on a Thursday evening. "Pick 'em all. Because Saturday, those folks'll be back."

I used to think of the whole road as his. With Jim gone, the road feels like mine.

One difference between me and Jim is that while I patrol the road's whole hilly mile, Jim never walked far. Sometimes he even drove the two hundred yards to our house. But on fine days, he did stroll about a bit, checking out our place and Duane's, making the rounds of the neighborhood like a dog. Bob and I do something similar, especially after we've been away for a few weeks. Bob prefers to go alone. I don't know his route, only that, as soon as we arrive from the city, even in the middle of the night in the middle of the winter, he has a walk he must take through our six acres before he can rest. I head first for the bridge, look upstream at our shoreline, then downstream into a wilder waterway dotted with little islands where ravens nest in snags. Often, Bob joins me here. But with or without him, the first thing I do in the morning is walk up the road a bit, to see who's here and sniff out who might have been, assess what's changed. When we arrive by day, I sometimes find, before I know it, I've gone the whole way to the farm.

Unlike Jim, I don't carry tools to clear fallen trees, and it never occurs to me to drive part of the way. But when Herman is expected for a visit, I always feel it's important to scout things out.

This was part of the reason I found myself walking up the road just after we'd arrived from the city one Friday last October. Bob was napping. I was tired, too, but the late afternoon light was glorious and I'd missed the road so much. And Herman was coming tomorrow.

All is peaceful. I see no sign of a vehicle, and at the farmhouse, everything appears to be in place, even Herman's curved stick propped against the screen door to keep it from flying open in the wind. Though I'd intended to go in and borrow a bowl in which to carry the cranberries I plan to pick on my way home, I decide not to, at least not yet. Maybe not at all, lest I inadvertently disturb something. Herman will be happy to see it just like this tomorrow.

I'm looking to my right, into the woods, as I walk on toward the barn, thinking maybe it would be nice to hike to the ledges tomorrow. Then I turn to the barn at my left and something within me freezes. The sliding door is part way open. Someone's been inside. I walk right up to the edge, where all grows dim, but don't cross the threshold. It's too dark in there to see whether Herman's lawnmower or any of the few tools he leaves there are missing. I'd expected to find something here to hold my cranberries, and on the dirt floor, there are, as usual, some old flowerpots, but they're so dirty I don't want to use them. I consider closing the door, but decide Herman should see it exactly as it was left by the intruder.

I'm calm inside again. The moment of alarm has passed. I turn my back on the barn, walk a few steps toward the woods, and stop to study the two or three bearing apple trees that remain in the field. The apples are quite ripe, many on the ground, and a trail made by a large mammal winds between them and beyond, through the high, matted grass, into the vastness of the forest where Bob and I got lost. A bear? I look and look. Apples. Trees. Grass. The fall air smells delicious.

And then I turn around and see, framed in the open loft window of the barn, a man.

He is dressed in dark camouflage, bow and arrow poised, his elbow on the windowless sill of the aperture. He is still as a portrait. So perfectly still, I wonder for half a second if I've conjured him out of the woods, the colors of the day, some place in me where still resides a thirteen-year-old girl willing to believe an enchanted forest could produce a comely and compassionate male companion.

Our eyes lock

"I hope I didn't frighten you," he says quietly.

"No," I reply. "I'm a friend of the owner. He's told me hunters use the loft."

I'd had a small startle reaction when I'd seen the open barn door a few moments ago, but I had none now. It was as if I'd recognized the man, though he didn't look in the least familiar. His face was handsome, kind, a full face, with regular features, dark eyes, thick black hair and a neatly trimmed moustache. The bow and arrow didn't scare me. Would I have felt different if he'd had a gun?

Yet I chose my words carefully, asserting my own right to be there, but also trying to make him feel at ease. *It's not my place,* I reminded myself. Herman carried on his family's longstanding attitude of open access. Neither the land nor the buildings were posted. His family did not hunt but it was tradition that hunters were welcome, even to store their beer in the cool of the well and hoist it up with a rope. He liked the place to be used, didn't even mind if strangers sought shelter in the farmhouse, as long as it was used with care.

"Did you walk up?" I asked the hunter, realizing at once that this was foolish. If he shot something, he'd need a vehicle to get the heavy kill out of the woods.

"No, a friend drove me and dropped me off." He explained that he was visiting from downstate. "He'll be back for me at dark."

"So, have you had any luck?" I'd never talked to a hunter before. Was that the right thing to say?

"I had a few shots, but I didn't take them. It's just an excuse to be out in the woods. It's such a beautiful evening, I figured I'd stay here until dark, just enjoy the beautiful evening, then go on down."

Evening? I thought. Is it evening? I'd been thinking it was afternoon.

"Have you seen anything?" I asked.

"A couple of deer in the distance, but I didn't try to get them. Though I could have. And turkeys."

I told him about the flock of a dozen or more that had wandered by our bedroom window a few weeks ago.

"There were no turkeys here for years, but they've come back. And the deer are back, too."

"Back? I didn't know they'd gone…."

"Before these woods were logged, there weren't so many. It's the understory plants they eat." That made sense. But I'd never thought of it before.

Even as he spoke he remained motionless, frozen except for his handsome face.

It's often been said that, at least in this part of the world, humans are the most dangerous animals in the forest. Bob and I were acclimated to fear hunters. At least half a dozen times we've found ourselves in the line of fire, even in our own front yard. Equally often, I've heard people claim that hunters are among the forest's best custodians. Am I willing to believe that perhaps some are?

The man tells me he's been coming here each fall for many years. "I don't really care if I get anything," he adds. "It's an excuse to be outdoors. Soak up the quiet."

I tell him about our cabin down the hill, and that I come here often, too. He's a prison guard, he says, goes on to talk of how stressful his job is, the renewal he feels spending a few hours here, in a place so remote from his everyday that it feels like a different planet. "Makes me human again."

Of course I know exactly what he means.

Slowly, as we talk, I become increasingly comfortable. Though I come to this lonely, beautiful place empty-handed, and he comes with bow and arrow, we share the serenity of the mild fall dusk, the rich complexity of the autumn smells of life and decay, the beauty of the sky, the awe for the vastness of the forest. We accept its invitation to reflect, and the gift of transcending, at least for a moment, our separateness from this world. We release ourselves to imagine we can blend, invisible as the specks in the universe we truly are, with all the other creatures of the wood.

I awoke the next morning with his image in my eyes, framed in the barn's open window, benign as the constellation of the hunter Orion, harbinger of winter, in the sky.

Today, when I am so soon to leave, the image of the hunter in Herman's barn reminds me that land doesn't really belong to us. Each time we leave, we give it back to the forces of the weather, to the other creatures who were here before us and who will be here, I hope, when we're gone. And to neighbors and strangers, to protect or violate. We may claim ownership of the logs and stones and boards and metals of our buildings, but the forest goes on to live its own life.

August 25

What sort of day is it? If I can't sort it out, I'm out of sorts. When the weather can't make up its mind, I can't settle mine to task, but jump from one project or idea to another, move from room to room, in house and mind, hoping the sun will emerge.

In the last fine days of summer, I see the season's end everywhere in the angle of the light: the backlit birch; the way the sun begins to drop behind the trees at four o'clock, taking the temperature down with it through the still-bright afternoon.

How I will miss the mornings—the birch tree with the sun in its leaves, the shifting sky, the sounds and the silence, which are essentially the same here. The stream carrying the mood of endless possibility into the day.

People sometimes ask what it's like to go back. More often, they say, "I don't understand how you can go back."

Here's what it's like: I am the katydid that came to town by accident on the flowers I picked just before we left last September: pink and orange zinnias, purple coneflower, violet harebell, golden-glow, black-eyed Susan, salvia, white goose-neck loosestrife, crimson bee-balm from outside the back door and trailing red verbena from my window boxes. The katydid apparently rode on the back seat for nearly six hours in this mobile garden, then jumped off the bouquet to find herself on metal—the trunk of the car where I'd set the flowers for a moment.

I stand at the curb, guarding against a ticket for double parking, while Bob brings the flowers and the heavy boxes of our summer's books upstairs, and watch the katydid. Gingerly she places her feet on the hard, slick surface. Her legs are no wider than a piece of sewing thread and surely not half as strong. Her small head keeps turning, looking around, I think at first, but then I realize more likely she's feeling her way through this new environment with her antennae, three times the length of her body, and covered with tiny sensory receptors. She's a nocturnal creature and these receptors enable her to find her way in the dark. It occurs to me that she might have been asleep all day among the flowers, only to wake up here. Poor thing! She makes her way rapidly, but with purpose, not panic, across the trunk of the car, as if certain she'll find a place to get more comfortable, and determined not to stop moving until she does. The leaf-shape of this insect, mistress of camouflage, is vivid against the dark car. Her color is the intense, almost iridescent light green of spring foliage. I get a better look at her than I'd be likely to in the country. So, of course, will her potential predators.

There's a pathetic flower bed under the gingko tree next to which Bob parked. I pick a pachysandra leaf to see if I can get the insect to crawl onto it, but she won't. I try the coleus. She rejects that, too.

A katydid, I recall ruefully, is a close relative of the grasshoppers I've been fighting all summer with dish detergent, garlic sprays, cayenne pepper and expensive nematodes ordered from Nebraska, as they ate the goldenglow, an old-fashioned perennial, tall and stunningly prolific, hard to replace. By night, this katydid might have dined on the same flowers I saw her red-legged cousins chewing on by day. Yet, here, I feel obligated to protect her. I don't want to capture her in a jar, though I will as a last resort. But when I pluck a half-dead blossom of white chrysanthemum from the flower bed,she jumps onto it without hesitation. I quickly put the blossom down among the other mangy mums.

For a moment I watch the unlucky insect try to acclimate, hop from stem to leaf to flower. There is nothing tall here, it is nothing like the overgrown perennial bed from which she came. The katydid is so perfectly adapted to a garden like mine, wildflowers flourishing with cultivars, a thousand places for her to sleep discreetly through the day, passively evading her many predators. How easily she could succumb here to a pigeon, a dog, a heavy human foot. But it's all I can do. For a time, at least, she may avoid becoming some other creature's meal by changing color to match her surroundings. I believe she has it in her to become gray as the sidewalk or brown as the bare earth that will soon be all that's left under the gingko tree, just as I hide my country self in the sleek black disguise that carries me around Manhattan.

I am not literally some other creature's meal, but sometimes, in the city, I do feel I am being devoured by those for whom I work. I have no reason to feel more vulnerable there, but I do. In the country, like the katydid, I have an abundance of places to hide. Each year, however, hiding becomes more difficult.

When we were househunting, we'd seriously considered "going off the grid" and buying a place where power and phone were unavailable. Of course our lives are infinitely easier with the services we've always taken for granted, but when we bought the cabin Bob and I agreed we didn't want to turn it into the electronic cottage. I spent my first summer here with only an electric typewriter and, as a backup, one of those ancient little Olivettis people use in movies when they're in Africa writing in a tent. Now we have an answering machine, fax, computers, printers, internet, VCR, cordless phone. A cell phone will probably be next, whenever the towers are built to provide service.

I don't want most of this stuff. My work options would be very limited if I were less accessible. Yet each time I log on to check email, I feel as if I'm walking out the door. My concentration is broken, I am less fully here. What Bob likes to call "the realm of commerce" used to mean an 80-mile round trip to Glens Falls. Now it's right here in the cabin, in a choice of two metal boxes. One morning last week, when Bob and I took a walk up to the farm, my first thought as I breathed in its spacious quiet was, *"No one can find me."*

The rest of the year, I want to be found, discovered in a slush pile or a magazine that has my byline. I want the phone to ring, the email to flow, feel nervous if there's no buzz around me. I love working on projects with other people, where constant communication is part of the process, though I often resent the need to interrupt myself to check email many times each day. And I hate the noise.

Bob and I live in the high-ceilinged, two-bedroom apartment I rented for myself and my daughter when I left the Hamptons and my marriage. At the time, I didn't give a thought to whether it would be quiet. The house I'd left, set right on a major road, wasn't so quiet either. So now I live and work with a constant hum of traffic, frequent sirens, garbage trucks, hourly church bells, jackhammers when some utility is ripping up the street.

Listen. It is not so quiet here. Birds call in the woods, insects hum nearby. Occasionally there are distant rumblings, faint and hard to place. Yet I bask in silence.

There are many different kinds of noise, the worst of which is generated by my mind: anxiety, worry, my wonderful habit of berating myself for past failures and mistakes. The most deafening noise of all is the inner voice that wonders—whatever I'm doing—*shouldn't I be doing something else?* When I am here at the studio, even if I am merely staring at the stream, that voice is still.

And what should I be doing here? In spite of myself, I've let the reins of necessity fall slack.

I come here with one huge, audacious expectation: to open my eyes to the day, set out on a path, sit with pen in hand, open a book, or just sit and stare and say "Tell me a secret."

Now, at summer's end, I'm the child who hasn't had enough time to play outdoors, who doesn't want to go alone into a room to practice the violin.

Of course I cleave to this place because it's here that I've learned to do the opposite of everything I was taught: not to complete a task but to chase after a bird instead, not to exercise vigorously but to stand or sit still for a long time and watch a tree or listen to the stream or watch the water flow... or less, even, than that.

It's much easier for Bob to navigate the country city transition than it is for me. "The difference between us," he said yesterday, when I told him how much I dread going back (which of course he already knew), "is that we don't return to the same city."

Though he's far more likely to complain about his job than to say something positive, Bob loves teaching science to inner city teens, despite the poor skills and overwhelming problems of many of his students. He always refers to them as children, though none are younger than fifteen. Some live in shelters, some have lost parents to AIDS, a good number are already parents themselves. Most have friends or family who have succumbed to stray bullets or substance abuse or who are, rightly or wrongly, incarcerated. Always grumpy and tired, he struggles to bring the best of himself into each day. He is constantly researching and creating new curricula, which gives him the opportunity to read and study to his heart's content. If you catch him at a good moment, he'll admit he loves his students, and on one of his best days, might even admit that they love him. Here, he's always alert for what he can bring back to them: plants, rocks, lichen, pond water to examine under the microscope, seeds to experiment with, photos he's taken of the night sky.

At summer's end, Bob knows what he's returning to. For me, it's often a *tabula rasa*. Each year, my need for this place strengthens my commitment to my freelance life. This means I return each fall to a different job or no job at all.

In a good year, there's an editorial job in an office. Unlike most writers I know, I don't mind the constraints of office work. I enjoy the routine of being expected somewhere, in fact, I prefer it, from time to time—to be with other people, have a set routine, feel my work is complete within certain hours, escape from the wilderness of writing and the muddle inside of my own head. That I thrive on this activity and on conviviality makes me in an important way unsuited for a writer's solitary life.

Whatever my city work, I quickly shed my country skin and grow a new one. I get a good haircut, meet friends for coffee, pound out emails and work the phone. None of which distinguishes me from millions of others. When I work at home, piles of papers and books sprout like woodland mushrooms after rain on every surface, in every room. Some days are so crammed I have no time for lunch or breakfast. One weekend, from his favorite perch at the exact center of the apartment on the living room couch, surrounded by his own piles of books, Bob looked up from the pages of *The Secret Life of Dust*, and having observed me for a while as I buzzed from one project to another, commented, "You were a blur."

But no one really knows me until they see me in the country. Without makeup. With my uncombed hair in need of cutting, with an unabashed tan, charging into underbrush, heedless of poison ivy, chasing some new plant. One September, an acquaintance, after telling me how great I looked, asked me *sotto voce* if I'd had a facelift.

Though, more than ever, I live two lives, I no longer think about which life is my real one. The more at home I become in the wilderness and the cabin that is our bridge to it, and the more intimately I know it, the more it meshes, inextricably, with the other, what I used to call my "real" world. Back in New York City, I will think about the mice in the cold cook stove, the house creaking and settling all alone, the leaves dropping from the red maple near the driveway. They will all be gone when we come back. I don't think about the city ever, at all, when I'm here. Apart from friends I stay in touch with there, it ceases to exist for me. As I ride the subway or stride down a busy street, I'm as likely to ponder the activities of beavers or coyotes as those of my human fellows. It's the life of the forest that I dream about in my city bed. When I consider distances in city blocks, this road's landmarks are my measure. The conversion is guesswork: Is that shop as far from this street corner as the farm is from my driveway? Is the walk to that office building longer or shorter than the walk from the cabin to our property's edge at the main road? If I'm tired and think a distance long, I put it in the country and it shrinks.

"You have the best of both worlds" is another thing that's often said to me. I'm not sure there is such a thing. Sometimes I feel I'm neither here nor there, and don't live either life completely. The need for this duality is something I've been blessed or cursed with. But this bifurcated life is what I choose.

Yesterday I found myself thinking, *Other people have secure jobs and money. I have this.* And a great blue heron flew past me down the stream, silent as a kite.

August 26

I didn't think we were going to have another warm day, but here it is, the sun that has nearly made me the blonde I was as a small child.

Nature is full of surprises. Not all of them nice.

A downy woodpecker tells me the trees around the studio are sound as he flies or hops from one to another, sampling the permeability of the bark. First the big red pine at the south corner of the deck, then the cedar near the north corner, below, then the balsam next to it: tap tap tap. Tap tap tap. Finding no insects to eat, he silently wings into the woods. But half an hour later, as if recalling something overlooked, he's back, on a mission, checking that red pine again, scaling the hundred feet of its trunk, tapping here, tapping there. He has a feeling, an instinct for a meal in this tree. I must doubt its soundness now.

Observing subtle changes here reminds me of the truism that every moment really is new and different. If we could fully appreciate all the nuance of that, perhaps we'd never be bored, or even as unhappy with our lot as we may have plenty of reason to be. In the city, I find it impossible even to hold this idea in my mind. There is always too much that is new and different. So much that it can feel like too little.

And there must be a way, too, to wake up each day and fully feel the newness, the endless possibility, in the familiar person on the adjacent pillow.

As everyone knows, most living creatures play out a pattern of mating rituals when they first come together. It's also true that many—birds, mammals, fish, insects—engage in ritualized behavior with their chosen mates throughout their lives. Scientists have identified hundreds of monogamous bird species that sing the same duets over and over again as long as they both shall live. Surely coupled humans are similar. Over time, like most people, Bob and I have become increasingly entrenched in habit: habits of response, as well as ways of doing things in which we take comfort, or behind which, perhaps, we hide. I wonder how the birds and animals feel about the patterns they enact with their mates. Do they ever find them irritating? I know we do.

"I knew you were going to say that," I hear too often from Bob.

I knew you were going to do that, I hear in my own mind when he raises the radio volume on some classical warhorse I'd prefer not to listen to at all.

Still, we've gotten better at switching parts in our duet. The other day, at the post office, I became utterly distracted by a friend's invitation to go off looking for wild orchids, though Bob and I had set aside the day for end-of-summer chores. "We have to consider our priorities," Bob said, to my surprise, assuming the voice of reason I tend to think of as mine.

And, as we did when we were lost, we seem to manage adversity by making such shifts that ensure we're never both at a complete loss at the same time. We've memorized each other's lines, take turns applying logic and asserting some clear-headed, reasonably optimistic view. The emotional weather varies more often with a subtle breeze than winds of change. And yet I wouldn't trade his constancy for anything. He is my bedrock and I hope I'm his.

And there's something else: When Wendell Berry writes of care for other species, he says, "Care allows creatures to escape our explanations into their actual presence and essential mystery." Bob understood from the beginning that this is part of what it means to care for another human being, and he taught it to me.

August 27

I awake at dawn and see from the back window that the hillside has been attacked by a marauder. The bear again? A moose? In the night he broke the lower branch of the beautiful young mountain ash and bent the trunk. He dug up the monkshood I planted yesterday, uprooted the petunias, ate the Jacob's ladder down to the stem.

The empty bird feeder lies on the ground, still attached to its wrought iron post. I rush out barefoot, in my nightgown, to survey the scene at closer range. And there in the pale light is my marauder: a placid doe.

Still browsing the hill, she steps as gingerly through the brush as I step on the scruffy lawn on naked feet. She's still interested in the ash tree but doesn't really care for it, tasting the branch she's broken off, then tossing it aside. Lifting her head, she gives me a level glance, only mildly curious. We observe each other for what seems a very long time before she ambles on her way.

If what you relish in life includes the unpredictable, along with the wild turkeys outside the bedroom window you take the *derecho*, the deer that eats flowers, the bear at the door. I right the bird feeder and refill it, then, hoping to discourage the deer when next she comes round, I go into the house, snip off a few locks of hair at the nape of my neck, and scatter the hair at the base of the ash tree's slender trunk. Looking at it on the ground, I see that my hair is the same color as hers. Can she see this, I wonder? And I find myself hoping not that she'll be repelled enough by the scent of my hair to leave the tree alone, but that she'll recognize me as kin.

August 28

I look for things to look forward to in the city. I come up with only two: a bathtub and Chinese food.

Back in my apartment, there's all sorts of stuff I don't need and don't miss. It's fun, in a way, to return and see what's there, most of it as forgotten over two short months as the contents of a trunk locked in an attic for years.

Over time, I expect I'd miss the instant gratification of Manhattan's Upper West Side with all its greengrocers and flower markets. In September I luxuriate in the Friday farmer's market, the squashes and lettuces and herbs and roots, the subtle spectrum of the apples—from green through merely blushing to vituperative red. The peppers are my favorites: purples, yellows, vermilion, even white. I buy them for the visual surprise, arrange and change them in baskets, observe their hues in different lights.

Why do I need to go to the city to admire fresh vegetables? The only local produce you get in our part of the Adirondacks is what you grow. Most people have gardens, but this close to the high peaks, the soil is so thin, the season so short, those who might have farmed even a generation ago just aim to grow enough for home. Still, by the end of August, gardeners are alert for folks who can use some extra tomatoes and summer squash. "What do you call a woman who buys squash at the supermarket?" asks my neighbor Betty. "A woman who has no friends."

Once I have a bathtub, I don't think Chinese food and convenient shops will be sufficient to make me look forward to the return to urban life. And while I wish that bathtub were already here, right now, it's work to adjust to the idea that this is our last summer in the tiny cabin. It will still be a log cabin, and not large, but in addition to a decent bathroom, we'll have a larger kitchen, an extra room. Closets! I hope this will not encourage me to bring more of what, until now, I've left behind.

The hardest thing to say goodbye to is the studio, even harder than the garden and the birds and the stream. I came here today to pack my books and my work. Instead I've merely listened to the water, cascading through the woods after yesterday's rain. The studio is a place of summer and packing up my work means summer's gone. Still, I'm learning that I can accommodate the loss in leaving. I've long understood that leaving is part of the forward motion of life. Now I see that forward motion is not necessarily linear: it can include return. As Jim left, in an aspect, I became him. As the farm's iconic qualities dimmed with the cutting of its trees, they blossomed in our cabin. It is no longer the farmhouse, but the cabin, my own place, that is my dreamscape.

August 29

Two days before we are to leave, Herman comes for a last visit of the summer. He's bought a comfy new little Jeep and, before dinner, he drives us up to the farm. The roadway, despite Ernie's efforts before the logging and all the events, known and unknown to us, that have transpired on it in these few years, is much the same as when we first saw it: pocked and pitted, cobbled here and there with stones and boulders dredged from its shoulders, where the town highway department periodically carves a drain. For roads like this, as for the people who persist on them, each season, on its unique terms, can be a challenge to survive. After even a moderate rain, the surface from the bridge to the farm is a web of rivulets, a map of the moon. Riding in the Jeep, we all agree it would be easier on our bodies—and far more pleasant—to walk.

August 30

And walk we do today, all the way up to the ledges, the place Ernie called "the looking rocks." The way is so different now; I couldn't possibly find it on my own. But even with all the landmarks gone, Herman has little difficulty learning his way through the forest again.

The three of us stay up there a long time, on the rounded surface of granitic gneiss, a great elephant hide of an outcropping, staunch and crusty with half a dozen kinds of gray and brown lichens, sculpted by a glacier 10,000 years ago. Every little pocket of depression in the rock is filled with piles of soft brown pine needles. We gaze at Gore Mountain, Moxham Mountain, and beyond, and down at the valley, where the first of the trees have already taken an autumnal turn. The reds and yellows make the many shades of green even more beautiful, the lime and chartreuse of the late-turning aspens and birches, the evergreens' intense, mysterious darks.

It's windy, and I take refuge behind the fat trunk of a white pine, won't even go as far as the middle of the rock where Herman is standing. Bob, cigarette in one hand, camera in the other, is out at the edge, as usual, taking a photograph. The three of us are mostly quiet in our happiness in the moment. When the wind dies back, it's silent except for the tree frogs shrilling among the foliage. After a while, Herman steps a little further back on a narrow strip of rock to talk to me. He and his brother plan to sell the farm eventually, as I've long known. But there's been no decision yet about whether the family will keep the old house, or some other part of the property. "It won't happen soon," he assures me. Then he tells me a wonderful secret:

"I come here all the time," he says, "in my mind."

"So do I," I admit.

"Sometimes I climb up here to the ledges. But mostly, I just take a walk on the road."

"That's what I do."

"And I think about how it's just a path cut through a wild forest more than a hundred years ago. And what it was like for the people who lived here then."

My mind is blank. I want to hold on to what Herman's just said, try to leave this open space for whatever may come to fill it.

I'm not quite ready to tell him, or anyone, that I wonder if Jim and Ernie—separately, of course—still walk here, too. And that I wonder about the others, unknown to me, who made and may still make this their secret place. There are footprints on the road sometimes, along with tracks of fox and deer, and the feel, now and then, of those who leave no tracks at all.

August 31

We won't be here for the groundbreaking, to see a machine take the first bite out of the earth. So, at six this morning, in a mousy nibble, I took the bite myself. First I plucked the bird feeder's wrought iron stand from the ground where the new space will be, and moved it a little way up the hill into the woods. Then I plunged my spade into the earth and dug up a red spruce, about two feet tall, that had taken root under the feeder, no doubt seeded by a bird. I put the tree in a bucket and carried it, along with my big transplanting spade, across the bridge. Giving in to an impulse I've fought too long, I planted the tree on Duane's side, in front of the deteriorating old gray picnic table by the stream, facing our little beach. I didn't tell Bob.

This act, I know, is proof that I have yet to persuade myself to leave the natural world to its own devices, much as I believe I should. What I've really wanted to do is to invade Duane's with seeds by the pound and plant wildflowers—bigger, more plentiful and more colorful than those that have found their way there on their own.

But what I want most right now is for the work on our cabin to be over—all the disruption that's about to begin. I'm torn between wishing I could be here to witness every moment, and being grateful to avoid the intrusive reality of the heavy equipment, the digging and uprooting. I have yet to be blessed with the ability to wait serenely for things to come full in their season or even the sense to try.

I will never become one with this place until my ashes are scattered in and around Trout Brook. I hope they fall to land where potash-loving fireweed will grow, and that some who pass will appreciate it for what it is: not a weed, but a wild flower, with a color that illuminates the landscape, and apart from picking a few stalks to brighten a bouquet, will let it stand to lose its petals, form a seed head birds or wind will scatter, and bloom again somewhere.